EFFECTIVE COMMUNICATION AT WORK

A practical guide to strengthen communication skills, empathic listening, conversation and dialogue skills to be successful at work.

LIAM HARRIS

D1522075

TABLE OF CONTENTS

INTRODUCTION _____ 1

1 – COMMUNICATION AT WORK _____ 5

1.1 How to improve communication at work _____ 6

1.2 7 Top Tips For Better Workplace Communication _____ 10

1.3 The Importance of Communication at Work _____ 13

1.4 How Staffing Organizations Can Help _____ 14

1.5 Reduce Conflict and Improve Communications at Work and Home ____ 17

1.6 Communication Process _____ 18

EXERCISE _____ 21

2 – DO YOU UNDERSTAND EMOTIONAL INTELLIGENCE? _____ 23

2.1 Benefits of Emotional Intelligence _____ 28

2.2 How To Increase Your Emotional Intelligence _____ 29

2.3 Emotional Intelligence - A Conscious Solution _____ 30

2.4 Negative Impact on Business _____ 31

2.5 Developing Emotional Intelligence Skills _____ 32

3 – WHAT IS THE IMPORTANCE OF EMPATHY? _____ 33

3.1 On the Absence of Empathy - And What to Do About It _____ 36

3.2 The Importance of Empathy in the Workplace _____ 39

3.3 Tools For An Empath's Energy Protection _____ 40

3.4 Characteristics of An Empath _____ 44

EXERCISE _____ 48

4 – WHAT IS SELF-AWARENESS _____ 51

4.1 Self Awareness, the Key to Finding Meaningful Work _____ 52

4.2 Being Self-Aware and Emotionally Intelligent to Reduce Workplace Stress 54

4.3 How To Develop It Self-Awareness _____ 56

EXERCISE _____ 63

5 – LEADING PEOPLE THROUGH CHANGE _____ 65

5.1 Change Unity Model _____ 65

5.2 The Strategic Planning Group _____ 67

5.3 The Group of Facilitators _____ 68

5.4 The Implementation Group _____ 69

5.5 Collaboration, Communication, and Capability _____ 70

5.6 Is Your Leadership Effective? _____ 71

5.7 The foundations of a strong organization are: _____ 72

6 – CONFLICT MANAGEMENT: 6 TIPS TO SUCCESSFULLY MANAGE DISAGREEMENTS AT WORK _____ 73

6.1 Common Reasons For Team-Building_____ 75

EXERCISE _____ 84

7 – ALWAYS THE VICTIM AT WORK? WIN WITH FEEDBACK ____ 85

7.1 The meeting's fourth stage is to end on a positive note. _____ 88

7.2 Maintain Self-Control and Get Positive Feedback _____ 89

7.3 Useful Tips for Giving Good Feedback to Staff _____ 89

8 – FIGHT FEAR OF SUCCESS AND FEAR OF FAILURE! _____ 97

8.1 Fighting Fear_____ 99

8.2 Remove the Fear of Taking Action _____ 103

EXERCISE _____ 107

CONCLUSION _____109

INTRODUCTION

"What is communication?" is a question that many people ask. That is a big question. Most of you, I'm sure, have an idea and might explain your own perception in some way. But, based on my research and writings, the best summary I've come up with is as follows:

The act of transmitting or exchanging information, signals, and messages through verbal and nonverbal activities is known as communication. It is a system of sending and receiving between humans by way of speech, writing or technology within our personal and industrial lives.

What is the meaning of communication? It's impossible to stop at one paragraph. It goes beyond psychology and physiology, neurology, and electronics to contribute to human contact through communities, countries, and continents.

Telephone, telegraph, radio, television, transportation, and shipping are all examples of communication as a means of sending and receiving information. Technical communication, company communication, online communication, and communication in the context of efficiency are all examples of "what is communication?" questions.

What is the meaning of communication? From the microelements on Earth to the macro elements in space, our entire universe is one big ball of technological and human communication.

Individually, communication is a never-ending system of transmitting or exchanging information, signals, and messages through verbal and nonverbal activities that begins at birth and continues until death — both before and after.

However, in its most basic form, when it pertains to human communication, it is a sending and receiving mechanism that often necessitates the presence of a Sender and a Receiver. It's difficult to connect with oneself. But there is a lot of that going on in your head and your self-talk.

Animals can also be communicated with. People, on the other hand, need other people to interact on a human level. And it occurs on a two-way street platform where a sender and receiver exchange communication-specific codes.

Have you ever been curious about how the body interacts with one another? How does it go from being given an order or a stimulus to executing a physical or emotional reaction?

Let's paint a mental picture by taking a brief look at psychology.

To put it another way, within the body, messengers (neurones) obtain an order (a stimulus — for example, hitting your big toe on the baseboard), pass it on to other neurones along with the nervous system, who pass it on to yet other neurones, who finally make the connection to the muscles to be contracted and deliver the ultimate response (retraction of the foot from the painful sensation).

The nature of the above mechanism is that it involves various types of messengers (neurones), each of which carries a particular substance (neurotransmitters) to bind the original stimulus to the ultimate reactions.

The messengers in communication are the events that take place during the communication process; the stimulus comes from the sender, and the answer comes from the recipient.

The "connecting force" between the messengers or the events taking place between the two individuals is critical when all of this occurs.

It's like the gear coupling in mechanical processes; it's like the keyboard between human fingers and the computer screen; it's like the machine driver between the screen and the printer... or the receiver and transmitter on an electronic circuit board...

The gears will not work together if the coupling is incorrect. If the keyboard is malfunctioning, the screen will show garbled scripts or none at all, and so on.

The funny thing is that our nervous and neural systems' neurones already know what to do; the unconscious mechanism is built-in. However, we must learn the "rules," which are the equivalent of "neurones" within our bodies to communicate in a conscious verbal and nonverbal manner.

"Physical comforts cannot subdue mental suffering, and if we look closely, we can see that those who have many possessions are not necessarily happy. In fact, being wealthy often brings even more anxiety."

Dalai Lama

1 – COMMUNICATION AT WORK

Fixing stuff is said to be a male characteristic. If you tell a man your problem, he will try to solve it; if you tell a woman, she will listen and empathize. It's nice to lend a hand, and most of us want to do so. Fixing, on the other hand, carries three risks:

- I might fix it before I fully comprehend
- What works for me might not work for others
- If anyone solves my problems, I might not learn to fix them myself

What someone needs isn't always what they require. If someone tells me they have a "time management" problem, I might enquire, "How do you know you have a time management problem?" just to make sure we're on the same page. "Because I'm always overworked, behind on assignments, and late meeting deadlines," they might reply. As a result, we move on to determining the root cause of the issue, which may include everything from working procedures to technological skills to external circumstances to difficulties in saying "no."

They might have expected me to teach them time management or prioritization tool before we met, but we quickly discovered that a combination of better working habits, enhanced delegation, a few PC shortcuts, and a new degree of assertiveness combined to effectively overcome the issues.

The Slim Business Communication Model is a set of steps - or a method - to adopt in specific work scenarios, and it can be used in both group and one-on-one conversations.

Supporter with a mindset of "how can I help?"

Listener To assist, I must first listen and comprehend the situation.

Influencer Once I comprehend the situation, I will begin to influence it.

Motivator, and I will then assist in motivating all parties involved to take action. When it comes to working experiences, it's common to start with good intentions but then jump from "S" to "I" before fully comprehending the situation. Another bad habit is that after ideas have been exchanged (the impact process), we don't contribute much to the inspiration phase if we haven't used our own ideas. As a result, SLIM necessitates a positive mindset, a desire to get to the root of the problem, a willingness to give of oneself, and the discipline to follow through and complete tasks. Everything well and good in principle, but sometimes difficult to put into practice!

There are three major situations in which SLIM can be effective:

The Job Interview - that is, to show that you have a thorough understanding of the company and its problems, to assist them in keeping and gaining customers, and improving the customer experience.

The Customer Interface is a must-have for dealing with customer complaints.

The Performance Appraisal is useful for both appraisers and appraisees.

In reality, SLIM is an important aspect of work culture on a broad level, whether it's walking to someone's desk or work area to discuss a problem or giving someone time when they enter your workstation.

1.1 How to improve communication at work
In all areas of life, good communication is essential. That is to say, something that involves two or more individuals.

Let's look at an example that isn't related to work for a moment.

Consider two people going on a holiday together.

You can imagine the many possibilities of this trip if it is planned and undertaken without effective communication.

Tickets can be forgotten, planes and trains can be delayed, double hotel reservations can be booked and paid for, and so on.

Such a trip has the potential of being a disastrously memorable experience.

However, with good communication, the vacation can turn into a fantastic adventure that will be remembered fondly for the rest of one's life.

Good communication isn't something that just happens.

Planning, coordination, checking in to make sure it's working and recognizing - or even celebrating - progress are all necessary components of communication.

Consider what needs to be changed in each of these stages of an efficient communication process if you need to enhance communication at work:

PLAN FOR SUCCESS

1. Remember, first, what your communication goal really is.

Communication that works well is:

- Engaging
- Customer-focused
- Easy to use
- Enough, but not too much
- Effective

2. Be prepared for your communication to be complete.

Good communication conveys several things about a shared effort or experience.

Be prepared to provide the following information:

- When it is happening
- What is happening
- Why it is important
- Who is involved
- How the work or event will occur

3. Be aware of your audience.

Find out who they are if you don't know who they are or don't know anything about them.

What you communicate and how you communicate makes a huge difference.

4. Determine what the information's intended use is.

People receiving and using the information may need less detailed information if they only need to be aware of something rather than taking action.

5. Communicate in a way that allows the audience to clearly understand what you're doing.

Some audiences prefer to communicate through the internet, e-mail, or text.

Others need face-to-face contact for their messages to be answered effectively.

For information to be completely absorbed and actionable, certain interactions necessitate a community phase.

6. Make a plan for how you'll ensure that communication is being received.

Many managers send critical information without double-checking that it was received.

It's critical to ensure that important information is received correctly, particularly when communicating with others.

This may include questionnaires, interviews, findings, or other methods of determining if the message was received or not.

Make the required preparations.

VERIFY... THEN CORRECT, IF NECESSARY

7. Check to see if your message is being sent.

Don't take it for granted.

Check it out.

Also, keep in mind that one-time contact is often insufficient.

For example, if you're talking about a big change or important action that needs to be taken, one rule of thumb is that you should do so seven times, in seven different ways, to ensure that the information reaches everybody who needs it.

Consider this: you've done it seven times, in seven different ways.

Knowing this, you won't be shocked if you have to send a message again or in a different format to ensure that it gets through.

8. Improve the communication that hasn't yet been effective.

Improve or fix communication that didn't work or didn't work as well as it should have for those involved to take the corrected or desired acts.

PAUSE TO CELEBRATE WHEN IT WORKS

9. Pause and notice that the communication worked, when it does.

Also, acknowledge the people who were involved in making the process successful.

EFFECTIVE COMMUNICATION AT WORK

10. Review and reflect so that you can repeat success.

If this was an especially big communication effort or an especially important one, take some time to review what worked and why.

Pay attention, as well, to what didn't work, and why that happened.

Record the information so you can use it again.

There's no need to reinvent a process that works. And there's no need to repeat a process that didn't.

Good communication is not effortless. Often, it's not easy.

That's why communication, when it works, is often worthy of quite a celebration.

1.2 7 Top Tips For Better Workplace Communication

Do you believe that words are the primary form of communication? What if you discovered that nonverbal contact accounts for 70% of all communication? That is, your body language, which includes your gestures, eyes, and even hands, speaks more often and loudly than your words. For organizational leaders, the ability to communicate clearly and effectively is a must-have skill. Here are some key ways to improve the efficiency and effectiveness of your contact.

1. Provide clear information

Workplace communication aims to pass information from one person to the next. If your communication isn't complete and accurate, it may create more uncertainty than clarification. Plan your correspondence carefully to ensure that you are passing along the correct information and the appropriate amount of information so that those with whom you are talking understand what you want to say.

2. Be truthful about your communication.

When something doesn't add up, people notice. If you attempt to communicate something that isn't completely real and truthful, it will be discovered. It's difficult to maintain dishonest contact in the workplace (or anywhere else) because keeping all of the stories straight becomes too difficult. Rather than saying things that aren't really real, say less. If it's not real and truthful, speak the truth and leave the rest for later, or don't say anything at all.

3. Bring non-verbal and verbal communication together

Keep in mind that contact can be both nonverbal and verbal. An individual can say one thing but behave in a completely different manner. It's not unusual, for example, to hear someone say "Yes" but shake his head horizontally, indicating "No" nonverbally (in the US culture that is). This sends contradictory messages. Make sure your non-verbal and verbal communications are in sync to get your contact together.

4. Listen

Listening is a crucial communication skill that is seldom practiced well. You must be able to hear what is being said to actually exchange information with another person. You'll be able to react to the actual message this way. The majority of conflicts are caused by a lack of listening skills. Take time to repeat what you hear from the other person to help you learn how to listen well. To ensure consistency, simply paraphrase what you said. This would significantly reduce friction and improve the quality of your interactions.

5. Ask questions

Questioning is a good way to double-check what you've heard so you can react appropriately. When you ask questions, you give the other person the opportunity to explain what they've said. It also helps you hear an answer differently or simply hear it again to make sure you heard it correctly. Be certain that your questions are relevant to what is being said.

Don't interrupt the conversation with a question about anything completely unrelated. Use questions to quickly collect additional information that will help you understand the discussion.

6. Allow others to talk.

Have you ever been in a meeting where only one person spoke the whole time? Some even go so far as to pose a question and then answer it? Few things irritate me more than when someone takes over a conversation. At the very least, a conversation is a two-way street. Remember to allow others to talk. Even if you have a lot to say, dominating a conversation turns it into a monologue rather than a dialogue. Solicit feedback, ask for responses, and include others in the discussion. Often all it takes is a few moments of silence.

7. Engage in Difficult Conversations When necessary

Do you ever put off saying what you need to say or stop having a tough conversation? A circumstance will not go anywhere if you remain silent. Instead, things seem to deteriorate. In certain cases, not interacting will add to the tension and trauma of a situation. Rather than avoiding uncomfortable conversations, sit down and prepare what you'll say. It's a good idea to jot down the key points so you can feel confident in what you're saying. To encourage input from the other person, make sure your tone is transparent and non-confrontational. Conversations aren't always enjoyable, but having the words out will help to ease stress and allow the situation to progress.

1.3 The Importance of Communication at Work

Communication is one of the most important aspects of a productive workplace because it influences employee efficiency, cost-effectiveness, and innovation. Here are a few examples of how communication is important in the workplace:

Setting Clear Workplace Expectations

Managers will send their teams understandably instructions if they have good and direct communication. There is a lower risk of errors due to misinterpretation if workplace rules and standards are accurately described. To be an effective leader, you must know how to use communication to motivate your team, establish consistent company policies, and provide appropriate project guidance.

Strong Relationships with Coworkers and Customers

Excellent communication facilitates the development of good working relationships as well as relationships with customers. Communication that is based on meeting individual needs, offering positive feedback, and conveying useful knowledge boosts confidence and loyalty. Strong internal partnerships can also help with efficient customer communication, accurately identifying goods and services, and clearly establishing organizational principles. As an employee solves a customer dilemma, good communication often aids effective problem-solving.

Promotes Innovation

A sense of community is fostered by effective organizational communication, which promotes creativity and innovation. Employees who have a good understanding of their company's priorities will concentrate on finding places where changes can be made to enhance the company's performance.

EFFECTIVE COMMUNICATION AT WORK

Employees are more likely to contribute ideas if they believe their feedback is important. To stay open and receptive to this input, business leaders must have excellent communication skills.

Cost-Effective

Organizations may lose money due to ineffective communication. Employees who have communication issues may need more training to help them communicate with customers and colleagues. If an employee's communication is a persistent problem, the organization will decide to fire them. This is an additional cost, as companies lose money by getting a vacant position and then having to pay for hiring.

1.4 How Staffing Organizations Can Help

Communication is an essential tool for fostering cohesion and efficiency in the workplace. When communication breaks down, it affects employee retention and efficiency, as well as company profit and innovation. One way to assist in the creation of an efficient and profitable workplace is to use skilled staffing services.

Through carefully screening candidates before you begin hiring, these career specialists will assist you in recruiting successful communicators who work well as a team. Some staffing firms also provide workplace management services, which assist companies in recruiting and managing specific departments.

Communication Skills - More Than Talking The Talk

You've probably heard the phrase "communication is key," And nothing truer has been said! Every relationship in your life, whether it's in business, at work, or with your family, requires effective communication. Let's concentrate on only one of these topics right now: workplace communication.

If you deal with other people, you've also had both positive and poor contact experiences. The advantages of effective communication are numerous. You can get more done in less time with good, direct, and respectful communication, and it also helps to foster a culture of respect.

On the other hand, bad communication causes tension, anger, misunderstandings, and dishonor, as well as affecting the company's bottom line (which, in turn, kills your earning potential).

Different aspects of communication are often overlooked in our daily lives. Although some people believe they are excellent communicators, they are almost certainly missing something. What is the reason for this? And in most places, excellent communication skills are simply not taught. So, when you read through these steps, don't say to yourself, "Wow, I've never had that problem," or "I'm a great communicator!" Because the truth is, there's always space for improvement! And as your ability to communicate improves, so will your earnings! That is a proven truth. So, start looking for ways to develop your communication right now. "Where am I falling short in this area?" ask yourself.

The tone of voice: "It's not what you say, it's how you say it," as the saying goes. The tone of voice may convey either honor or disrespect. It has the ability to convey either trust or fear. We don't always understand how we communicate with others. So, pay close attention to how you speak and interact with others today.

Are you respecting your bosses? Can you respect those who work "below you" in the organization?

Nonverbal communication: So many people are unaware that nonverbal communication accounts for 93% of all communication. If you're sitting back with your arms crossed and not smiling, your body is saying, "I'm not interested in what you have to say. I don't want to be here. I don't want to listen to you." If you're smiling, sitting forwards, and participating in the conversation, your body is saying, "I'm interested in what you have to say. I don't want to be here. I don't want to listen to you." The other person is more receptive, which draws you into the conversation even more.

Clarify: Don't say you know exactly what everyone is talking about. "So what I hear you saying is...," you can use to double-check that you understand what they're saying. Since you're essentially recapping the conversation, it makes you pay attention. Simply ask, "Can you explain that for me?" or "What do you mean by that?" if you don't understand anything.

Follow up: ALWAYS follow up! Follow-up is a key part of communication that, unfortunately, many people never do. However, it's as easy as sending an email after a phone call. This involves providing feedback on tasks or assignments that you are working on. Following up with the supervisor, colleagues, and teammates keeps everyone in the loop and informed about the situation. It also removes the need for them to track you down to see where you are or what you're up to. When a team's lines of communication are available, productivity soars and a harmonious work atmosphere emerges.

Here's the thing: one of the most valuable skills you use daily is communication. However, if you have bad communication skills, the chances of success are slim. However, if you keep focusing on developing this specific skill set, your performance will increase.

So, once again, take a few minutes today to consider how you can enhance these four areas of workplace communication. Later on, your bank account will thank you!

1.5 Reduce Conflict and Improve Communications at Work and Home

Every day brings a new set of challenges. Any of these challenges, if not all of them, can be used to strengthen our ability to adapt and contribute more effectively to the world around us. "In every crisis lies the seed of opportunity," says an ancient Chinese proverb, which one of my good friends introduced me to. If we approach crises with the right attitude, they can also make us stronger, kinder, and help us cultivate greater compassion towards others.

Controlling my ability to respond impulsively when disappointed or uncomfortable with a situation or others' reactions has been one of my biggest challenges in life. When others intrude into our personal space, are indifferent to our needs, or ignore our personal boundaries, most of us become enraged. Under these cases, I had a lot more trouble showing self-control or regulating my ability to self-regulate when I was younger.

Although I have significantly strengthened my ability to be positive, the environment continues to present obstacles, and it is difficult not to respond at times. Even now, there are moments when I am dissatisfied with my answers, and I strive to be more accepting of myself, respectful of others, and less critical of my flaws. I'm much stronger at not responding to strong emotions emotionally than I am at reacting to strong emotions externally in tough circumstances.

I believe that our unreasonable expectations of ourselves, as well as our excessive self-criticism, make it difficult for us to react effectively in difficult circumstances. We are unlikely to have a heavy emotional charge if we are attacked by another and have little or no self-criticism about the other's remarks. On the other side, if we are extremely critical of ourselves in one area and someone else targets that area, we are far more likely to become unproductive and emotionally reactive. Learning to thank ourselves for our efforts, strengths, and abilities can be very beneficial from this viewpoint.

Developing a greater sense of self-acceptance will assist us in avoiding becoming reactive as well as the negative energy directed towards us by others.

The ability to reframe a situation is likely to have a big effect on our actions and our ability to learn from a bad situation. It is not always the situation that determines how successfully we manage many problems, but also how we view the situation. It may be enough to cultivate the confidence that a situation may be a learning opportunity or experience in and of itself to help us deal with the situation more effectively. We are in a much better position to benefit from our experience if we chose to concentrate on our actions and behavioral reactions rather than trying to influence the other. Let's face it, we do not influence other people's actions. We do have the ability to regulate our actions, which will most likely alter the dynamic between us and others.

1.6 Communication Process
How Communication model works?

According to the communication model of Shannon-Weaver, the process of communication flows through 8 different steps. These steps include source, encoder, message, channel, noise, decoder, receiver and feedback. The sender or person who initiates contact to express his message, ideas, or thoughts is referred to as the source. The encoder will choose the interpretation format in which the message will be sent to the channel. The message is the sender's or source's idea, inner feeling, or perception. The channel determines how the message will be sent, whether it is verbal, nonverbal, electronic, or anything else depending on the needs of the sender. Noise is described as something that interferes with the transmission of a message, whether it is a physical or psychological barrier. The message would be decoded based on the receiver's desires and ability to comprehend the message.

The receiver is the person to whom the sender wishes to communicate, and he or she will eventually react in the form of input about how the sender's message was received.

Effective communication is described by another well-known author, James Humes, who says that "the art of communication is the language of leadership." Only when the recipient fully understands what the sender is trying to convey, whether verbally or orally, does communication function. Not only does face-to-face contact work, but body language and gestures also clearly communicate the sender's messages. Many obstacles, on the other hand, become restrictions in the communication process, preventing people from being communicated effectively.

Physical, social, mental, and psychological obstacles can all be encountered. People's ability to communicate is hampered by non-attentive listening. Community, language, context, and thoughts may all function as roadblocks to successful communication.

When people interact with one another, their language and culture matter. Similarly, some people break emotional bonds with one another, causing them to become distracted from the main subject. Since people or receivers may not feel at ease with the speaker's language, vocabulary, or sound, the method of communication plays an important role in the process of successful communication. Communication from afar can be difficult for both sender and receiver since some people are unfamiliar with technology and others are distracted by background noise or other factors.

Tips for successful communication: The sender should explain his message before passing it on to the recipient. He must use appropriate words, terminology, and communication networks. Active listening is required on the receiver's part because many obstacles can be easily removed if he listens while staying active. Similarly, communicators must cultivate empathy so that they are aware of one another's emotions and thoughts. The sender's movements and body language must correspond to the messages he or she wishes to express.

Similarly, both the sender and the receiver should first consider their respective calibers (such as history, culture, and language) before proceeding. Communicators must give each other a chance to express what they want to say so that they can all explain it. Respect must be present during the dialogue phase for it to be successful.

"Communication is a skill that you can learn. It's like riding a bicycle or typing. If you're willing to work at it, you can rapidly improve the quality of every part of your life"

Brian Tracy

EXERCISE

WRITE DOWN 10 WAYS COMMUNICATION HAS HELPED YOU MANAGE DIFFICULT SITUATIONS AT WORK?

2 – DO YOU UNDERSTAND EMOTIONAL INTELLIGENCE?

Emotional intelligence is a valuable skill because it indicates that you understand and get along with a wide range of people. Once you recognize emotional intelligence, you'll be able to see who has it and who doesn't at work, in politics, in the media, and in your community. Both EI and EQ (like IQ) are used in the media as abbreviations for emotional intelligence.

Empathy is akin to emotional intelligence. It's the ability to "sense" and react appropriately to other people's emotions. Emotionally intelligent people excel because they develop strong bonds with others and are loved and trusted. People trust you and learn to depend on you when you know how and when to be sympathetic, helpful, straightforward, and trustworthy or gentle with them. This establishes a foundation for business and personal interactions that leads to the development of long-term, fruitful relationships.

You must learn to concentrate not only on your own wants and needs but also on the wants and needs of others, to build emotional intelligence. This necessitates the development of delayed gratification, persistence, and consideration for more than just profits. Emotional intelligence is also known as emotional maturity, which refers to the ability of your mind to control your emotions. The five attributes of emotional intelligence, according to Goleman, are self-awareness, self-regulation, motivation, empathy, and social skills.

• **Self-Awareness**: People with high EI are aware of their emotions, and as a result, they do not allow their emotions to control them. They understand the distinction between feeling and thought, and they may use thinking to moderate emotions rather than suppressing or dismissing them. They're optimistic because they trust their instincts and sound judgment, which comes from assessing circumstances through emotions and rational thinking. People with emotional intelligence are able to look themselves in the eyes and see themselves objectively. They are aware of their strengths and limitations and seek to improve in these fields. They have really positive self-esteem, which means they set rational expectations for themselves. They care for others, but they aren't dependent on them. They have the ability to set limits for their own self-defense. EI is built based on self-awareness.

• **Self-Regulation**: This capacity to regulate thoughts and desires is also known as self-control or impulse control. People who self-regulate are less likely to become enraged or jealous; they are less likely to have temper tantrums or hysterical outbursts; and they are less likely to make rash, reckless decisions. They consider their options before acting or reacting. Consideration, the ease with transition, honesty, and the courage to say no are all characteristics of self-regulation. They understand the value of deferred gratification and that waiting for what they want can yield better results. They follow an internal code of ethics rather than an externally defined standard of conduct.

• **Motivation**: People who have a high EI seem to be inspired. They're able to put off instant gratification to achieve long-term success. They're extremely productive, enjoy a good challenge, and are extremely successful at what they do. They realize that celebration and gratitude inspire others, and they are able to motivate themselves and others when the situation calls for it.

• **Empathy**: The capacity to connect with and comprehend the wants, needs, and perspectives of others. Empathetic people are excellent at understanding other people's emotions, even though they aren't apparent. As a result, empathic people are typically good at handling relationships, listening to others, and responding to them. They reject stereotypes and fast judgments, and they live their lives openly and truthfully. They display benevolence and kindness, as well as a good attitude towards others.

• **Social Skills**: Another sign of high EI is good social skills. They know how to work together and work as a team. Rather than focusing on their own achievements, they recognize that success comes from assisting others in developing and shining. They are skilled at resolving conflicts, communicating effectively, and establishing and sustaining relationships. People with high EI are also good at tolerance, kindness, trustworthiness, gratitude, compassion, and are emotionally sensitive, in addition to the empathy on which these social skills are focused.

Here's how to say if you or anyone else has emotional intelligence:

1. What is one sign that an individual has no EQ at all?

He or she has no idea how to respond to an emotional comment or question. "How do you feel about...?" elicits only his or her thoughts, if any.

2. What are the disadvantages of relating to someone who lacks emotional intelligence? It's not really satisfying, but we all want to be able to understand and empathize with others' emotions. It also implies that the individual would be incapable of listening to or empathizing with your situation.

3. Can we keep our distance from anyone if we can't sense any emotional intelligence?

It's going well if the relationship is going well. This is a pointless question. If you're frustrated by a lack of emotional intelligence but everything else is fine, you might try to teach it to a friend, parent, or partner, but patience is needed. It's like trying to describe emotions to a three-year-old.

4. What if the individual has some emotional intelligence (EQ)? What would you do to assist them in gaining more EQ?

When his or her EQ is on show, be very sensitive and helpful. If he or she does something thoughtful, make sure to thank them. Praise her or him if she or he listens sympathetically to you or anyone else.

5. What can we do to inspire others to remain emotionally aware and intelligent?

Make an emotional connection with him or her. Don't be impatient; it's not very emotionally intelligent. Give him or her space to react emotionally and thoughtfully to you.

6. Why is it desirable to have a high EQ?

In your relationship, high emotional intelligence fosters intimacy, warmth, empathy, and love. With someone who has a high EQ, having fun and sharing feelings is easy. An individual with a high EQ is likely to be kind and considerate.

To develop emotional intelligence, do the following:

Perform the following steps before engaging in some new experience or activity:

1. Make a mental note of the possibilities: Is there something you can learn there? Is it possible for you to make a new friend? Will just getting out of the house and meeting new people be beneficial?

2. Remind yourself of your objectives: you're going to meet new people and have a good time.

3. Think about your good personal qualities: What do your peers think about you? What is it that you admire for yourself? Your wit, your sense of humor, your personal style, and your ability to converse? Are you a considerate and loving individual? You will radiate your good energy if you remind yourself of these qualities.

4. Have a positive attitude: Studies indicate that people who have a positive attitude live longer, partially because a positive attitude is appealing and appealing, and people are attracted to it. As a result, you meet new people.

When you are optimistic, you are accepting of yourself and others, and you consider the positive aspects of life rather than the negative aspects, making it easier to communicate with others. You still feel a lot better about yourself, which makes you feel like you're more worthy of friends. It's an optimistic spiral that keeps going up.

5. Be fascinating: Wear clothing that is both attractive and interesting, and that represents who you are. Wear a shirt, scarf, tie, or jewelry from another country if you enjoy travel, or something that represents your ethnic heritage or a hobby if you enjoy traveling (sports, the outdoors, a Hawaiian-type shirt with surfboards, gardening implements or an animal print). It will help at the beginning of conversations. Make an effort to match the motivation to that of the people around you. Obviously, the energy level would be high whether you're dancing or enjoying barbeque poolside. The energy would be more mellow and concentrated if you're having quiet conversations at a cocktail party, discussing books, taking a class, or sitting down to dinner.

6. Pay attention: Take a look around and make friends. Take note of who's in your immediate vicinity and what interests or attracts you about them; then find something fascinating about what they're wearing and compliment it. "Excuse me, but I couldn't help but notice the lovely color; it suits you perfectly." alternatively, "What a fascinating timepiece! Is there a plot to it?"

7. Prepare ahead of time: Read up on some interesting topics to discuss, such as the behind-the-scenes of a hit movie, a cutting-edge technological advancement, or a hip new trend. Then you'll have plenty to say when someone approaches you.

8. Find a way to help: What tasks do you think you'd enjoy doing? I suggest having a "job" to do if you're in a new setting. "What can I do to help?" isn't enough. Instead, volunteer for a particular task, such as greeting guests and showing them around, keeping the food table stocked, or refilling beverages. It will give you a sense of belonging, provide you with an excuse to meet everyone, and keep you occupied enough to keep your nerves at bay. The host or hostess will be pleased, and you will be remembered.

9. Follow up: If you meet someone you'd like to get to know more, extend an invitation to coffee after the event or meeting. These social situations are where the best friendships begin.

Emotionally Intelligent conversations are like tennis matches. That is, the other person "serves" he or she asks a question or makes a statement. Then, you "volley" back you answer the question with the kind of answer that invites a response. For example:

He: "How do you know our hostess?"

You: "We went to school together. I like Pam's friendliness, don't you?"

2.1 Benefits of Emotional Intelligence

Have you ever seen someone who graduated first in their class and was extremely intelligent repeatedly fail in business? What about those other moderately intelligent people who are actually constructing empires and transforming the face of the world?

What about Henry Ford, for example? He never finished high school or college. Ford, for example, dropped out of school at the age of 15 and went on to amass a fortune and forever change the world. You may be wondering how this works and what emotional intelligence can do for you and your company...right? Here's how it works...

Many people's success has nothing to do with their IQ, but rather with what's known as Emotional Intelligence (EI). Merriam Webster defines emotional intelligence as "the ability, power, capability, or, in the case of the trait, trait, to recognize, evaluate, and control the emotions of oneself, others, and groups."

Emotional intelligence, to put it another way, is the capacity to perceive, appreciate, and function through your own and others' emotions. Higher levels of insight, compassion, empathy and the ability to effectively interpret these emotions are also advantages of emotional intelligence. These factors can make or break a small business owner's success because business is all about relationships.

Negotiation, for example, always necessitates the ability to listen, comprehend where a person is coming from, put yourself in their shoes, and then come up with a creative solution that benefits all parties. This cannot be achieved solely through book knowledge; emotional intelligence is needed.

Emotional intelligence also aids you in comprehending, anticipating, and navigating the needs of others. When interacting with clients, prospects, suppliers, business partners, and even employees and contractors, this is quite useful. You'll be way ahead of the curve if you can make everyone around you feel respected by anticipating and controlling their expectations before they even know they have them.

For instance, if you can determine that your target group has a desire to belong and expects or hopes that your company will make them feel that way, you can devise strategies to address this, such as launching a membership site.

The advantages of emotional intelligence in business are much too many to mention. Many have already been listed, but here are a few more for your consideration. Consider where you would be able to bring it in. What do you excel at and where do you have space for improvement?

- ✓ Trust your business instincts and intuition
- ✓ Listen to others, understand them, and make them feel appreciated
- ✓ Deal better with conflicts
- ✓ Solve problems quicker
- ✓ Offer better customer service
- ✓ Control your reactions to challenges, and stay positive when mistakes happen
- ✓ Market to your customer because you're better able to empathize with them
- ✓ Write better, more emotionally driven, content
- ✓ Connect with potential partners and build business relationships
- ✓ Hire the best people for the job

2.2 How To Increase Your Emotional Intelligence

Many people believe that intellect, whether it's IQ or emotional intelligence, is something you're born with and can't change. That clearly isn't the case! To boost your emotional intelligence, all you need is a desire to do so. Begin to observe how others behave, as well as how you behave and respond, and try to put yourself in their shoes. Learning to empathize is one of the most effective ways to start improving your emotional intelligence, and it has a significant impact on how you conduct business.

Take some time to examine your business relationships in light of the numerous advantages of emotional intelligence that I have mentioned in this post. Keep track of your own success. You might also devote one week to each aspect you want to change. You can do it, and given how important emotional intelligence is to your business success, I would get started right away!

"If we wanted to change the situation, we first had to change ourselves. And to change ourselves effectively, we first had to change our perceptions."

Stephen Covey

2.3 Emotional Intelligence - A Conscious Solution

By enhancing the Emotional Intelligence (EI) of its employees, an organization can successfully leverage two key trends identified in Patricia Aburdene's Megatrends 2010: "The Wave of Conscious Solutions" and "Spirituality in Business." As we enter this new era welcoming the widespread application of conscious techniques in business, ensure that your organization is an early adopter, reaping the benefits over your competitors who lag bogged down with traditional business beliefs.

Emotional intelligence is the ability to learn and apply information from your emotions and the emotions of others. It is a deliberate approach to knee-jerk reactionary emotional patterns. Knowing how you're feeling will help you make better choices about what to say or do (or not say or do).

It allows you to use your emotions to make better decisions at the moment and gain better control over yourself and your effects on others. The definition of emotional intelligence is based on brain research that shows these skills are distinct from technological and strictly cognitive abilities because they involve a particular part of the brain - the limbic system, rather than the neocortex - and involve a different part of the brain. There are five fundamental competencies that makeup Emotional Intelligence. The first step is to understand how you're feeling. The second is dealing with your emotions, especially those that are distressing. Self-motivation is the third skill, empathy is the fourth, and relationship management is the fifth.

The Business Case[1]

Emotional Intelligence abilities are critical to individual and organizational success[2,3] The effects of Emotional Intelligence have been discovered to be profound, affecting a variety of business/people problems, including increased creativity and innovation, increased competitiveness, enhanced decision-making, and increased income, according to research. When we understand that the feelings that leaders, managers, and consumers experience have an influence on decision-making, mental clarity, and the bottom line of businesses, as well as the efficacy of government and non-profit organizations, the business case for improving emotional intelligence becomes apparent. The environment and culture of a company are influenced by the feelings that leaders feel. Leaders' feelings, in particular, affect how workers feel, how happy they are, how loyal they are, and how effective and successful they are. As a result, how workers feel and conduct their jobs affects how consumers feel, how happy they are with both goods and services, and how loyal they are to the business or organization. And a company's bottom line and profitability are directly influenced by customer loyalty. It's worth noting that leadership is at the heart of this series of connections. CEOs, Executive Vice Presidents, and Directors are not the only ones who lead. Every person in charge of a work team, every boss, and every employee in the company is a chief. One of the most critical aspects of ability growth is self-leadership. Self-leadership is the internal capacity to guide yourself to make the right choices and decisions at the moment, whether at work or home, during the day.

2.4 Negative Impact on Business

Examining the impact of unmanaged emotional reactions and lack of emotional intelligence skills reveals the significant, negative impact on business. Unmanaged emotional reactions or lack of emotional intelligence skills by executives and employees at all levels can lead to ...

- lack of innovation and creativity

---

[1] Daniel Goleman, Emotional Intelligence, Bantam Books, 1995
[2] Daniel Goleman, "What Makes A Leader?" HBR, 1998.
[3] Goleman, et. al., Primal Leadership, Harvard Business School Publishing, 2002.

- unsuccessful reengineering and process improvement initiatives
- slow development of high potential talent
- decreased productivity
- decreased customer satisfaction and customer loyalty
- career derailment
- high turnover
- stalled change initiatives
- declines in revenue
- increases in stress and healthcare costs
- negative organizational climate/culture
- workplace violence

2.5 Developing Emotional Intelligence Skills

The good news is Emotional Intelligence skills can be learned. However, there is a caveat: when we apply the typical training approach targeted for enhancing analytical or technical skills, we are doomed to fail. Conventional programs do not include the factors by which the limbic system (the emotional center of the brain) learns best: motivation, extended practice, and feedback. Developing emotional intelligence skills requires that individuals eliminate old behaviors and embrace new ones. And this requires practice and self-reflection on the impact of using the new skills.

3 – WHAT IS THE IMPORTANCE OF EMPATHY?

People who lack empathy seem to go through life without considering how others feel or what they may be thinking. Each of us has a unique viewpoint. We all have moods, feelings of pain and hurt, joy and sorrow. And when we only see things from our own point of view, we are severely restricted. It's quick to make assumptions and leap to conclusions without taking the time to assess another. This sometimes results in miscommunications, hurt feelings, tension, low morale, and even divorce. People do not believe they are being heard or understood.

A client indicated that listeners on a recent radio show were polled about how they knew they were loved, and they said they knew they were loved when they felt heard. People want to feel like their boss listens to them, according to employee surveys about what makes a good manager.

This is a major problem. The person feels respected as a human being when leaders, parents, and teachers listen, really listen, using empathy to consider what the person is thinking or experiencing without attempting to improve, repair, or solve their problem. People feel comfortable when they are valued. They have the impression that they are important. As a result, they are free to be themselves and do their jobs. In other words, when workers feel appreciated, they are more efficient.

The Power of Empathy

When you use empathy to figure out why someone is angry or why a child is acting out, you may discover that something happened at home that upsets them, such as their mother being ill or the child going hungry because there is no food at home. You should ask questions about someone's actions or emotional state instead of responding to their feelings or being defensive. While punishment or punishments may still be necessary, the individual will feel respected and heard if empathy is used first. As a result, they will be more willing to take responsibility for their acts.

In our communities, our classrooms, and our workplaces, empathy is the missing link. Kids can be cruel to one another as we get older. If we begin teaching empathy in elementary and middle school, we will grow up to be more caring, compassionate, and understanding of one another.

Compassion and Empathy

To be compassionate is to be concerned. It's the drive "to make one's pain go away." We must care to be empathetic, otherwise, the individual will not express their feelings. They would not feel comfortable confiding in us. We wouldn't listen to someone if we didn't have compassion. We wouldn't bother to enquire about their experience with them. We don't give a damn about what they're thinking or feeling. Compassion is a prerequisite for empathy.

Challenges to Empathy

What would it take to get a greater sense of empathy? Why don't we do it on a more regular basis?

For starters, it necessitates that we pay attention. We are always lost in our own thoughts and have our own agenda. We have a lot going on. As a result, we are unconcerned with what others are thinking or feeling. We need to be more self-conscious and aware of others to change. For instance, the next time you enquire about someone's well-being, pay attention to their answer. Do you think they're right? Is everything okay with them? Consider if you want to learn more. If that's the case, ask them a question or share an observation with them.

2. It will take some time. People in our fast-paced world just keep going. Empathy necessitates that we pause and pay attention. "What's the matter with you; you seem to be thinking about something?"

3. Your self-esteem is a hindrance. You won't be able to really be present for another person if your mind is preoccupied with negative thoughts about yourself.

> *"He who is not every day conquering some fear has not learned the secret of life."*
>
> *Shannon L. Alder*

People always believe they are empathic, but when you consider what you are thinking about while listening to the person, you will discover that you are preoccupied with yourself - how the person feels about you, whether they like you, that you should be doing something else, or that you won't be able to support them...blah, blah, blah.

4. There is history between you that you carry as baggage. The more time you spend with someone, the more history you have with them, the more difficult it becomes to set that aside and simply be with them. In order to fully open the link with this individual, you must be aware of and stop a preconditioned answer that you have created. Examine them with fresh eyes. Leave your belongings at the front entrance. Retell the relationship's narrative in a different way. This isn't going to be quick.

5. You're an expert problem-solver. You agree that if someone shares something with you, you are obligated to help them fix it. This is not the same as empathy. This is about you and your need to please or be right, not about them. It puts the burden of solving their dilemma on your shoulders instead of theirs. It demeans the person and makes them feel undervalued.

Empathy is a choice. We must make the decision to change, care, get out of our own way and bridge the differences that exists between us - generations, cultures, sects, socioeconomics, and so on. Empathy encourages us to be completely human while still allowing others to do so.

3.1 On the Absence of Empathy - And What to Do About It

Empathy deficit disorder is a condition in which a person lacks empathy. It's a fresh and disturbing disease that's afflicting Americans, and it's causing havoc on both individuals and society. What are some ways to recognize it and what steps should we take to remove it from our interpersonal relationships?

Douglas LaBier, a psychiatrist in the Washington, D.C., provides a few examples of people who lack empathy from his private practice. One is a husband deaf to his wife's complaints. Another is a technocrat indifferent to the long-term effects of global warming. A third is a financier content to dismiss the entire American Muslim community as "all terrorists anyway."

People who have experienced such blindness are unable to listen. They fail to understand that "we're all one, connected together," according to LaBier. We will "deepen [our] understanding and acceptance of how and why people do what they do and [we] can create respect for others" as we cultivate empathy, he says.

I assume LaBier is right, but there's more.

Empathy allows us to overcome ourselves by enabling us to bridge two disparate states of mind or states of being (ours and someone else's). It gives us the best chance of avoiding existential isolation and feeling like we have a place in the world with others. Find the following polar extremes:

Listening vs. telling. I cut myself off from learning things you and I have in common when I insist on my version of events over yours. Listening allows me to learn from (and about) you; ignoring you can cause you to become enraged and resentful.

Understanding vs. knowing. When I argue that only my truth is true and that your truth is incorrect because it is different, I am implying that my point of view is superior to yours—that I am superior to you. This concept is unlikely to appeal to you. Instead, I may accept the likelihood of two contradictory realities coexisting.

Accepting vs. judging. You and I are on the same level. I'm declaring you defective for being unlike me as long as I use statute, brute force, or other means to manipulate you—unless we agree on the terms. (Aren't all feeling states within the continuum of human ability when you and I disagree about something? After all, we're both humans.)

Adaptive vs. reactive behavior. If I insist that only my experience is right, I will have to continually defend myself against potentially dangerous suggestions from those who disagree. On the other hand, by integrating their perspectives into my own, I might be able to increase my chances of living and prospering in the world of others.

Individualists vs. globalists are two opposing viewpoints. The never-ending effort to defend my turf against literal and figurative assaults can cause me to neglect both positive and negative global developments. I'm missing out on a chance to build win-win situations. Cooperation, on the other hand, is critical in today's world.

Isolationists vs. communitarians are two opposing viewpoints. When I close myself off and concentrate on the tiniest possible description of my circumstance, I lose the comfort of those in similar situations. I really miss having the opportunity to reach out to isolated individuals who want to be a part of the group and can contribute significantly.

Long-term vs. short-term. I may lose the opportunity to see me and my endeavors in the light of not just my own life span but also posterity as long as I am self-absorbed and indifferent to the broader world.

Empathy helps us to stay on track in terms of time, place, emotion, and spirituality. It grounds us and gives us a sense of belonging. It feeds the belief system that we use to direct our individual and social lives. It enables us to embrace and accommodate ourselves and others, fostering diversity and recognizing everyone's right to a seat at the global table. It lays the groundwork for future citizens' global awareness education.

Perhaps most importantly, it allows us to build protection for ourselves while ensuring the community's responsiveness to everyone's needs in this age of terror.

3.2 The Importance of Empathy in the Workplace

Even the best nurses, however, can learn tools for improving their empathy. In fact, most people who score high on assessments in the area of empathy often have no idea what they do; they just know that they like people, they enjoy working with and helping people, and they value people as individuals.

In a recent lecture on empathy to healthcare professionals in New York City, the audience agreed that much of the time, healthcare professionals show empathy to their patients. When asked about using empathy for colleagues, relatives, or even themselves, the audience seemed confident that they could do a better job.

What exactly is Empathy?

Empathy is the desire to put oneself in another person's shoes. The quality of feeling and knowing another person's condition in the present moment — their experiences, feelings, and behavior (reactions) — and transmitting this to the person is described by positive psychology.

So you know what they're going through, or at least you think you do, and you share it to evoke further conversation or clarity.

Empathy is a skill in Emotional Intelligence (EI). There are four groups of competencies and eighteen competencies in the field of Emotional Intelligence. The four clusters are:

- Self-Awareness
- Self-Management
- Social Awareness

- Relationship Management

Empathy is a component of Social Awareness. This ability represents a person's ability to communicate with and relate to others, which is a necessary skill for forming and maintaining healthy relationships. Our relationships remain shallow and lack the complexity and richness that exists when we share an emotional bond if we lack the desire to understand what someone is going through. An opportunity has been squandered.

3.3 Tools For An Empath's Energy Protection

Common traits of an Empath and why they need protection:

Empaths are attracted to helping others and themselves. They are normally drawn to healing because they believe they have a lot of internal healing to do... before they understand that the majority of the healing needed is for those who they are intuitively 'feeling.'

They are usually exhausted all of the time. This is a major problem. People and their energies are continually invading the energy of an Empath. An Empath will normally take on too much and become exhausted quickly, and sleep or rest will not help. It goes much further and is very exhausting.

Empaths have exceptional listening skills. They really care for other people's well-being and sometimes find themselves listening to the woes of people they don't know. Empaths are very easy to open up to for the majority of people.

That's when they begin to spill all of the negativity in their lives. People are also unaware that they are doing so.

Since they care so much, an Empath would usually prioritize the needs of others over their own. People will normally selflessly lend their ear to support an individual, even if it is to their own detriment until they become relaxed enough with them to open up.

For Empaths, alone time is important. Many Empaths prefer to be isolated to disconnect from all of the feelings and energy that isn't theirs. It's time for them to reclaim their equilibrium and separate themselves from all external negativity.

Empaths may also have a moody personality. Empaths often seem to have huge mood swings, which may be due to the conflicting thoughts and emotions that they are bombarded with regularly. Not only are they bombarded with these energies, but they still have to sort through and find out all of the information that is being thrown at them.

They are highly sensitive to violence, abuse, and tragedies of every kind. Most empaths give up watching television and reading newspapers at some stage in their lives because they find it too overwhelming.

The ability to simply know is also a common Empath trait. Empaths also have knowledge of things they were never taught or told. This sense of understanding is not the same as intuition or a gut instinct.

For an empath, being in public places can be overwhelming or painful. Again, too many people's feelings can be picked up in public places when they aren't really trying. Most Empaths can stop this roller coaster at all costs.

Honesty and dignity are 'felt' by Empaths. They have the ability to say whether someone is being truthful or not, which can be very disturbing and painful in your life. It's much more disturbing when they're dealing with family members.

Feeling another's physical signs and pains. Many Empaths will experience an illness that is caused by someone else and has nothing to do with them. This is the pinnacle of empathy.

There are only a handful of an Empath's characteristics. Again, depending on the resources you use to defend yourself, becoming an Empath can be a curse or a blessing. Empaths can protect themselves in a variety of ways. One method is to avoid big social events or public areas at all costs. However, there are moments when you simply cannot stop them. As an empath, you can defend yourself in a variety of ways. Here's what I carry in what I refer to as "My Bag of Tricks": Crystals, meditation, and the White Light of Protection are some of the tools I use.

Crystals

Rose Quartz is an excellent crystal for Empaths because it promotes unconditional love and warmth through its soothing properties. This is particularly beneficial for someone who is harboring unloving energies from something, someone, or even themselves.

Empaths may benefit from black tourmaline or hematite crystals to help them remain grounded. These stones can also assist in the absorption of any harmful energy.

Malachite is another crystal that can help you absorb any unpleasant emotions you're experiencing, whether they're yours or not!

Labradorite is a crystal that protects your aura from consuming any problems that are shared with you.

Citrine is a yellow crystal that will help to lift your spirits. Citrine's soothing properties also include the ability to absorb negative energy from the environment.

Amethyst is another favorite of mine. It is not only lovely, but it will also improve your intuition. Increased intuition is beneficial to all, but it is particularly beneficial to Empaths because it allows them to know whether or not the emotions they are experiencing are their own.

Rainbow Fluorite is the last but not least. Rainbow Fluorite is the Mother of All Crystals for Empaths, in my view, because it benefits all aspects of being! This multi-colored crystal will assist you in remaining grounded to the earth, clearing and balancing all Chakras, and remaining attuned to higher dimensions.

These crystals are my personal go-to's for staying focused, grounded, safe, and tuned in. Crystals can and will assist you in healing your life.

Meditation

For thousands of years, meditation has been used to achieve a degree of consciousness that is beyond the limits of the everyday thinking mind. Simply put, it is the art of putting the mind, body, and spirit together!

Most people are unaware that our bodies were designed to self-correct to preserve good health by keeping mind, body, and spirit in harmony. Consider how possible it is to get out of control when the energy of others is constantly infiltrating your body. It's incredible!

Your life-force energy does not flow as it should when you are out of control. Aches and pains are symptoms of being out of control in life. When the body is out of control for a long time, it starts to cause sickness and disease.

Empaths will benefit from alone time and meditation to keep themselves calm, stable, and whole. Most Empaths place this practice of loving yourself at the bottom of the priority list if they even put it on the priority list at all!

White Light of Protection

I normally try to shield myself and my energy with 'White Light' when I can't stop doing things that don't peak my 'wow metre,' such as walking into big crowds. Many people approach it in various ways and there is no right or wrong approach because it is all about the power of purpose.

Before you do something, take a few minutes to yourself and relax in a quiet spot. Take a few deep breaths while closing your eyes. Visualize the white light of safety entering your body through your crown and filling your whole being with each in-breath. Continue to breathe in the white light until your whole body is filled with it.

Now imagine the light burning brightly and becoming so large that it now surrounds your whole body. Take a few minutes to sit and breathe deeply while feeling the light that surrounds you. Now smile and be grateful, because you've just shown self-love by prioritizing yourself. And you've just finished shielding yourself from all unwanted and disruptive energies in the environment!

If you have a sensitivity to other energies, these are only a few of the ways you can protect yourself. I hope this was useful! Please share any additional tips and tricks you might have that I haven't mentioned. Let's all work together to stay healthy and whole!!

3.4 Characteristics of An Empath

Empaths are people who are compassionate, caring, and willing to support others. They are also seen volunteering and serving others in emotionally taxing jobs such as childcare providers, medical practitioners, hospice nurses, midwives, and others. The majority of empaths arrived with the aim of healing humans, animals, plants, and the environment. Many healers have taken on so much external energy that they spend the majority of their time clearing excess energy and recovering from the previous episode that "blew their doors off."

Empaths who haven't learned to block out other people's feelings or control their own resources exhibit the following traits:

You're constantly overcome by feelings, and you're prone to crying uncontrollably, feeling sad, frustrated, or depressed for no apparent purpose. You may think you're nuts if you have erratic mood swings and bouts of unexplained exhaustion. It's like getting PMS all the time if you're a woman!

Unrestrained empathy may lead to symptoms that are close to those of bipolar (manic-depressive) disorder.

You walk into the store feeling amazing, but as soon as you enter the crowd, you feel down, frustrated, sad, or overwhelmed. You get the feeling you're coming down with something, so you go home and relax.

If you've discovered that being in public makes you feel overwhelmed, you might consider becoming a hermit. Even at home, however, you become depressed while watching the news and weep while watching a movie. When you see a Humane Society advert about animals in need of a sanctuary, you feel terrible. You could end up rescuing more animals than you can care for.

No matter who they are or what they have done, you feel sorry for them. You feel compelled to pull over and assist anyone who crosses your direction. Even if you don't have any, you can't walk by a homeless person without giving him money.

Many empaths are chubby. When they consume negative feelings, they can experience panic attacks, depression, and binges on food, sex, or drugs. To cope with emotional stress, some people can overeat or use their body weight as a shield or buffer. Yvonne Perry demonstrates how to use light as a form of defense in Chapter 9 of her book.

Most empaths can physically and mentally heal others by drawing the pain or ailment from the ill person and absorbing it into their own bodies. This is not recommended unless you know how to avoid becoming ill as a result of the procedure.

You may experience symptoms such as chest pains, stomach cramps, migraines, and fever without actually contracting an illness. You later discover that your "ailment" coincided with the onset of an illness in a friend or family member.

No one can deceive you because you are able to see through their facade and understand what they are really saying. You could also figure out why they lied.

People, including strangers, begin to open up and volunteer personal details. You may be sitting in the waiting room, minding your own business while waiting for your turn, when the person next to you begins sharing personal details. They never thought that you may not want to hear about their drama because you didn't ask them to. People may feel better after interacting with you, but you may feel worse as a result of their emotional distress being transferred to you.

Intimate partnerships are difficult for certain empaths. Since they are constantly taking on their partner's pain and emotions, they may easily get their feelings hurt, want to spend time alone rather than with their partner, feel vulnerable when having sex, and feel compelled to constantly recover their own energy when it becomes jumbled with their partner's. They may be so afraid of being engulfed by another human that they emotionally shut down to survive.

Many that are sick, struggling, or have fragile boundaries are attracted to an empath's unconditional empathy and compassion without even realizing it. You may have a horrible life before you learn how to block out the energies of others, in which case you may feel compelled to be completely alone to survive.

It's easy to see why being an empath is often very draining. No wonder that over time, some folks shut down their empathic ability. And, with that, they also shut down a vital part of their divine guidance system. Learn how to manage the amount of info-energy you receive and hear more of what is really important.

EXERCISE

WHAT COULD HAPPEN VS. WHAT WILL HAPPEN

When something is bothering you, it's easy to imagine the worst thing that could possibly happen. The truth is that these worries may never come to pass. What could happen is not the same as what will happen.

What exactly are you concerned about empathy?

Thinking of what could happen rather than what might happen will make you relax. When you start to worry, ask yourself these questions:

What are certain indicators that your concern will not happen?

What would most likely happen if your fear is not realized?

How can you deal with your fear if it comes true?

Will you be okay in the end?

How has your concern changed after you answered these questions?

4 – WHAT IS SELF-AWARENESS

Self-awareness is a process that involves becoming sensitive to, and responsive to, the many forms of feedback produced by both the self-system and the externally oriented systems within which one is embedded" Although being a very academic term, this one illustrates some key aspects of self-awareness. To begin, we must recognize that self-awareness is a continuous process; we will never be fully self-aware; it is something we must desire to improve; we must be receptive to it, and we must work on it. Second, it emphasizes the importance of striking a balance between oneself and the world, which involves other people - not too self-centered, not too other-centered. This balance also involves being in tune with oneself, not being too hard or gentle. People sometimes struggle with these kinds of balances.

As part of my research, I developed a method to quantify self-awareness based on this model and meaning. I developed, optimized, and validated this new measure after conducting numerous studies involving thousands of people. It consists of some questions with responses ranging from "almost always" to "almost never" on a seven-point scale. It's the first internationally applicable self-awareness test. This is the first step in becoming more conscious of your strengths and weaknesses, as well as any holes or blind spots.

Curious to know more... Continue Reading.............

"Worry a little bit every day and in a lifetime, you will lose a couple of years. If something is wrong, fix it if you can. But train yourself not to worry. Worry never fixes anything."

Mary Hemingway

4.1 Self Awareness, the Key to Finding Meaningful Work

Self-awareness is the secret to achieving productive work and fulfilling life. Knowing what you want seems to be an easy task, doesn't it? Is it, however, true? It takes time to get in touch with yourself by self-reflection. Gaining self-awareness is the first step towards finding successful work. Here are ten self-awareness issues to consider.

1. What are your strengths? What are weaknesses? Knowing your strengths and weaknesses will help you figure out what kind of work you'll be good at (that plays to your strengths) and what kind of work you'll struggle with (uses your weaknesses).

2. What is your vision for the future? What steps are you taking to achieve your goal? What do you think your life will be like in the future? A vision gives you a goal to strive for. To really get clear about your vision, you'll need some quiet time.

3. What are your values? Do the people you care for share your values? The attributes that are most important to you are your values. Some people will share your beliefs.

Others will hold different beliefs than you, but they will honor yours. Meaningful work incorporates the ideals and must be respected by your employer and/or customer/client.

4. Do you see yourself as others see you? Friends can see talent in you that you are unaware of. People sometimes believe that everyone can do what they are inherently good at. Others, on the other hand, might notice activity that is obstructing your progress. The DISC behavioral appraisal is a tool that helps people figure out what their visible behavior means about them.

5. What brings you joy? You are solely responsible for your own mood and attitude. Do you know what makes you really happy? Are you aware of when you're in a bad mood and do you have any methods for changing it? As your self-awareness grows, you know that staying upbeat and happy is entirely up to you.

6. When you were a kid, what kinds of things did you enjoy doing? We sometimes misplace anything significant from our childhood. Are you doing the stuff that used to make you happy as a kid? Reminisce about your youth and what you did for fun and pleasure. Is it true that you're still doing them?

7. What motivates you? Not everything we do at work or home is enjoyable or interesting. How can you get started on such time-consuming projects? Some people need assistance in being empowered in all areas. What gets you going in the morning? The Workplace Motivators evaluation will assist you in determining what drives your motivation at work.

8. What is your greatest fear in life? Knowing what you're afraid of and how to resolve or deal with it is crucial as you work towards your goal. You would be unable to step forwards in your job or your life if you become overwhelmed by fear.

9. What causes you to be stressed? Development necessitates a certain amount of tension. Burnout may be caused by too much stress. Some people's actions can change as a result of stress. When you're stressed, how do people see you? You may use the DISC behavioral evaluation to figure out how stress affects your behavior.

10. What methods do you use to communicate with others? What is your preferred method of communication? The majority of people can communicate with others in the same manner that they want to be interacted with. An individual who is outgoing and chatty may find it difficult to communicate with someone who is all business. The DISC behavioral evaluation will help you become more conscious of your own and others' communication styles.

4.2 Being Self-Aware and Emotionally Intelligent to Reduce Workplace Stress

So you want to reduce workplace stress, improve job satisfaction, increase productivity, and possibly advance your career. These are admirable objectives, and we should all be proud to help them. But what if none of these methods are effective for you? What are the solutions, and how can you de-stress and land the work of your dreams?

If you're going to college, you should be happy with yourself. You'll put in a lot of time at work, putting in 2000 hours per year for 40 years, totaling 80,000 hours. You don't want to be one of the 20 million people in the United States who suffer from a mental illness each year (includes depression, anxiety, phobias, etc). You don't want to be one of the 18.1 million people who suffer from dysthymia (chronic moderate depression) or major depressive disorder. So, what are some of the keys to a happy and productive workplace?

My first advice is to get to know yourself. Self-awareness, recognizing your skill set and knowing where you excel and where you struggle all aid in fitting into the workplace culture and expectations. I've previously discussed the importance of a good person-environment match, and I agree that people who do not have a good fit will be unhappy. Being depressed for 40 hours a week has many negative effects, including drinking, thrill-seeking (possibly by affairs or adrenaline-fueled outdoor activities), and destabilized relationships.

As a result, coming to terms with oneself in the workplace in a rational and non-depressing manner is an essential part of how we cope with job or workplace tension. After returning home from work at the end of a long week, I told my wife that while I am good at large-scale conceptualization, establishing research cultures and developing strategic visions, I am not so good at supervising administrative staff to ensure that they have attended to all of the requisite information and minutiae of my workplace. But I'll have to figure out a way to get around this so that my coworkers and bosses don't have to deal with my worldview.

Harvard studies and the work of people like Daniel Goleman fascinate me. I agree with research that suggests self-awareness and emotional intelligence are two of the most important performance characteristics that predict success. In general, I evaluate five aspects of an organization's performance: efficiency (which can be difficult to quantify in certain organizations), punctuality (and time on task), absenteeism (sickness, etc.), presenteeism (being at work but doing practically nothing), and staff turnover. Both of these factors affect work performance and satisfaction.

People with low self-awareness and emotional intelligence, especially leaders and managers, will struggle in the workplace. They can exacerbate rather than alleviate workplace tension. Their organizational units' efficiency would suffer. Absenteeism, presenteeism, turnover, and efficiency will all be higher. Those who work but do not supervise and are ignorant and emotionally dull build upward issues just as effectively as managers.

What does it mean to have high emotional intelligence (EI) or very high emotional intelligence (EI)? I'll use some material from a previous article because it nicely summarises why self-awareness and emotional intelligence are relevant. You probably have a very optimistic self-esteem, you are probably quite happy, you probably maintain good relationships and understand people very well, you probably manage life's challenging events and difficulties well, and you probably handle nearly all facets of your life very easily if you have high levels of EI.

So, you'd like to develop your management skills? Start by looking after yourself. By sitting down and conducting an audit of your personal and interpersonal style, you will reduce your stress, lower the stress levels of your partners, and reduce workplace stress for your coworkers. Solicit advice from a decent but frank and straightforward mate. Act on a personal development plan, as explained by your mate, to reduce the stress problems that seem to surround you.

4.3 How To Develop It Self-Awareness
[1] Pay attention to what it is about other people that worries you.

Things that irritate you about other people can often be a sign of an aspect of yourself that you despise, and therefore an area for you to focus on.

It may also be because they think and process information differently than you do, prompting you to reconsider and upgrade your understanding of their "type" [see 8. below].

When I consider those behaviors that irritate me in people I know socially, I've discovered that it sometimes touches on a part of my personality that I'm not comfortable acknowledging.

[2] Pay attention to what bothers other people about you

On occasion, you will meet and communicate with people who will take an immediate and intense aversion to you for reasons that are unknown to you.

I remember being disturbed a few years ago when I discovered that there was a man in my social circle named Mike who had a strong dislike for me. I was completely unaware of this at the time and only learned about it when another mutual contact mentioned that he was nervous about an upcoming social gathering because this man and I were both attending.

When I asked him as to why he was concerned he said: "... but Stephen, don't you know that Mike has real issues with you...?"

I had no idea what he was talking about, but it was later revealed that Mike disliked me because I was overbearing and arrogant. I was dumbfounded because I had no idea and couldn't remember any event or circumstance in which I could have acted in this manner towards him.

Mike's problems were on his side because he was responding to my optimistic and confident personality, and since I was an articulate confident salesman at the time, he felt intimidated by simply being around me...

The incident taught me to be more self-aware of how others would view me and try to be more sensitive as a result.

Years later, I've become painfully aware that simply being present in a room will elicit a reaction in people. I don't say this to be vain or self-conscious; rather, I've developed a degree of self-awareness that requires me to refrain from saying too much or, in certain instances, simply "bless them with my absence" in some social circumstances.

[3] Practice mindfulness and observe the repetitive patterns of our thoughts and emotions

Thich Nhat Hanh teaches us how to cultivate awareness by acknowledging that our true home is neither in the past nor in the future. The present moment is our true home.

Through mindfulness practice, you will realize that it is your relationship with your feelings, not the substance of your thoughts, that counts.

As a result, you will realize that you are not your thoughts.

[4] Know your emotional triggers

One of the advantages of mindfulness is that you learn to recognize when you are responding to your emotions.

I've been practicing mindfulness for about 15 years and can attest to the way it makes me become painfully and consistently conscious of my emotional trigger points.

For example, other drivers on the road who, in my opinion, are dithering and driving too slowly irritate me greatly. My responses are so predictable, but that is one aspect of my personality that I have yet to master control!

When it comes to bigger issues like relationships and business, I've learned to predict my reactions and not engage with my emotions, instead of letting them pass.

[5] Ask for feedback and listen

Choose someone you know well and who you can trust to give you objective input on yourself in particular circumstances.

I've asked my family and close work colleagues for input on occasion, and what I've found is that there's a disparity in how I think I'm relating to people and how they actually receive it!

For example, it's been said that I have a curt and bossy demeanor and often say things in a way that makes it seem as though I'm telling people what to do. In my mind, on the other hand, I still think I'm being really fair and supportive!

I understand that the issue here is one of tone. Clearly, my internal understanding of my communication style and how it is received are vastly different!

I can't say I'm perfect all of the time now, but at least I'm mindful of the issue and can try to correct it.

[6] Try different experiences - travel or learn a new skill

Visiting new and unfamiliar locations and getting outside of your comfort zones can reveal new aspects of yourself. This may be anything big like foreign travel or something as simple as picking up a new hobby and engaging with people who aren't your regular acquaintances.

Living in Singapore and traveling extensively across Southeast Asia, where I met, worked with, and socialized with people from a variety of backgrounds, has challenged and aided me in a variety of ways, and has certainly enhanced my self-awareness.

Despite our significant ethnic and cultural differences, we all have much more in common than surface differences might imply, and there is far more that unites us than divides us, contrary to what I expected when I first arrived in the area. We all have the same basic needs and broad expectations for ourselves and others we care for.

Living, working, and socializing under various political systems is initially difficult, and several of my previous "certainties" have been tested. One of the most important things I've realized is how narrow my initial experiences were. Observing life through the eyes of some of Southeast Asia's various regimes causes me to re-examine and reconsider some of my previous assumptions.

Vietnam is a good example. Spending time there and immersing myself in Vietnam's modern history and culture has drastically altered my perspective on communism.

I've always thought of communism as a negative force on a nation, and I'm old enough to recall when Ho Chi Minh was seen as a rabble-rousing communist threat in the west.

However, after witnessing firsthand the effects of years of colonialism, first under the French and then under the American War [as it is known in Vietnam], I can now see why Ho Chi Minh and communism were the "only display in town" at the time.

That is not to say that I now approve of or endorse communism; I do not; however, I can now see why it was perhaps the most effective tool for galvanizing opposition to western oppression at the time.

To any US readers who may find what I'm saying offensive, I respectfully suggest you spend half a day in Ho Chi Minh's War Remnants [aka War Crimes] Museum, where you can see firsthand the horrifying and long-lasting effects of US use of Agent Orange on the Vietnamese people, as well as the long-term ecological damage to North Vietnam's landmass.

I say "lasting effects" on people because children are still being born with horrific deformities as a direct result of their parents' genetic damage caused by the indiscriminate use of incredibly large amounts of Agent Orange.

It is estimated that between 1 and 1.5 million Vietnamese people are still affected. In modern Vietnam, there isn't a family network that hasn't seen at least one current-generation family member disfigured or disabled as a result of the use of this in the America/Vietnam war.

[7] Take psychometric tests

Take one of the well-known personality tests, such as the Myers-Briggs or Enneagram, to provide yourself with metrics and a framework for greater self-awareness and deeper insight into individual differences, especially in relation to how others think, react, and process information.

For me, this was a complete game changer! I couldn't understand how or why other people couldn't see what I could see, why they couldn't judge circumstances - particularly in business - and see exactly what needed to be done [or at least what I thought needed to be done] for many years of my adult life!

What a revelation it was when I discovered the Myers Briggs personality styles system one day! I could see with painful clarity how differently we all think and process stuff as I scrolled through the summary description of the main characteristics of the 16 forms. I have found that my dominant personality type is exclusive to a small percentage of the population.

So it's no surprise that I was always out of line with the majority of my peers when it came to thinking types. I recognize the absurdity of what I'm about to say, a businessman in his mid-forties finally understanding that most people don't think like him, but that was my truth.

Since then, I've tried to put in a lot of work into evaluating and accounting for these individual variations.

[8] Make time to clarify your values

Make time for self-reflection on the issues that are most important to you.

What brings you here? What are you supposed to do with your life? What makes a life worth living that you can be proud of?

I was recently sitting in a bar in Singapore with a group of ex-pat friends, enjoying some beers and catching up. When one of them asked the party, "What do you think?" the conversation took an interesting turn.

"If you knew you were going to die tonight and you were given a few minutes to reflect before that happened, what would you say was the meaning of your life?"

On hearing that question I suddenly had a moment of clarity and I realized that for me the answer was (and remains)

"What difference will you make? What impact will you leave in the lives of others?"

EXERCISE

WRITE DOWN HOW SELF-AWARENESS CAN HELP YOU AND HOW THEY AFFECTED YOUR MENTALITY BEFORE NOW

5 – LEADING PEOPLE THROUGH CHANGE

5.1 Change Unity Model

Working relationships can be stressful and frustrating, but they can also provide fulfillment and strength. Because of the limited time and resources available and the importance of implementation, one-on-one relationships are particularly critical in projects.

Every project stakeholder, but particularly change leaders, is responsible for maintaining harmonious working relationships. In this essay, many principles come together to provide a pathway to change unity, assisting change agents in becoming leaders and achieving unity for all individuals and teams involved in bringing about change.

The key to handling transition, according to a retired and formerly highly effective executive reported, was to clarify the priorities, keep everyone focused on them, and keep the momentum going.

As he led a large organization effectively for several years using this simplistic method, he added that it always surprised him how easily the weeds can grow and attempt to choke the plan; the weeds being distractions, interruptions, diversions, and the commotions that threaten progress.

The Change Unity model is an approach to setting goals and working together to achieve them that is both realistic and efficient.

To achieve goal consistency, there must be clearly established advantages, a future vision, and optimism for the future. Shift attempts stall if these aspects aren't clarified. People must be able to see themselves in the future, reaping the rewards of their efforts to reform and feeling secure in their future. These are basic human needs, and initiatives that do not meet them are doomed to fail.

Goals necessitate a daily attempt to refocus. Without such emphasis, goals fade in direct proportion to the amount of attention paid to the weeds. Couples who won't stick to the agreed-upon budget, families who won't stick to the agreed-upon balanced eating plan, and managers who won't stick to the agreed-upon company path will all succumb to Distraction and drift away to easier pursuits. Although "can't" is a real constraint, "won't" is an option, and the astute manager will make sure the everyday target refocus occurs.

The explanation for the refocus is straightforward. There can be no momentum without emphasis, and there can be no dedication without focus. The most common explanation for project failure is a lack of dedication and follow-through. Gym owners say that the majority of new registrations occur in January, following the most common New Year's Eve resolution of "lose weight and get fit." The initial flurry of activity in the first month is replaced with excuses why attendance is currently unlikely - as the credit card continues to subtract monthly fees.

Distractions 1: KPIs 0 on the scorecard

Commitment leads to momentum, which transforms a group of people who are only going to work every day into a team committed to achieving shared objectives. It's a manager's dream to see team momentum in action; it's a manager's nightmare to see self-interested individuals play power and politics and tear it apart. A well-coordinated team produces the energy necessary to achieve excellent results that always surpass expectations. People who, with accepted consistency and concentration, place their individual barrows aside and prioritize the team's goals overcome seemingly impossible obstacles.

The Change Unity Model applies the transparency, emphasis, and momentum principles to identify the basic stakeholders in an organizational change setting. It explains how each individual can contribute to the change unity needed to meet project objectives.

5.2 The Strategic Planning Group

The Sponsor has primary leadership responsibility for the project in the Change Unity Model. As a result, the Sponsor's job is to ensure that the Steering Committee and the program/project team understand the project's strategic purpose, are focused on the objectives, and maintain momentum across the project.

The Strategic Team achieves success by prioritizing constructive communication and the development of collaborative partnerships, as well as carefully weeding out discord and disunity. Although organizational reporting systems provide a foundation for project compliance, productive working relationships are preferable because reporting mechanisms are often insufficient to drive progress. Any project needs a Sponsor who can leverage through relationships, and Sponsors should be carefully chosen to ensure this capability.

Healthy transition starts by assisting stakeholders at this level to recognize that they are much better together than they are apart due to competing agendas. It's unfair to assume change solidarity in the rank and file if it doesn't exist at the project leadership stage.

5.3 The Group of Facilitators

The next line of responsibility is the Program Director, Project Manager, and Change Manager, who, like the Sponsor, concentrate on constructive communication and establishing working relationships with one another. The Facilitator Team achieves success by providing consistency to and among their teams, staying focused on the project's goals, and maintaining long-term momentum.

Careful weeding is expected here as well. Project teams can be a breeding ground for discord and, as a result, disunity. Team building, both inside and across teams, is a rewarding endeavor that pays off handsomely when it comes to project deliverables. This is the secret juggling act that produces the best results in the shortest amount of time while still adding zing to Friday afternoon cheer.

Projects have a propensity to delegate the "touchy-feely" stuff to the Change Manager, but project relationships are not solely the responsibility of the Change Manager: harmonious relationships are the responsibility of everyone.

5.4 The Implementation Group

Members of the Senior Management Team serve as the primary connection between the project and the company, and they are responsible for moving the project forwards in the business climate. Steering Committees are typically made up of the organization's senior management team, and it is their responsibility to ensure that the project is coordinated with other company operations, promoted among their employees, and that project benefits are realized.

They will provide clarification about the project, concentrate on the objectives and create sustainable momentum to achieve the goals, in addition to adapting it to the needs of the organization.

Their support for the Sponsor as a project leader, their executive alignment with colleagues, and their constructive promotion of the project helps the project. In a practical sense, the project benefits from management team support, inclusion in business schedules, and adequately equipped impacted stakeholders.

The last of the stakeholder groups responsible for working together against a shared purpose is the staff. If the previous stakeholder groups have succeeded in achieving consensus, the staff community would find it easier to do so.

Leadership and management styles, organizational structures and processes, power and politics, and human resource management strategies all contribute to the formation of cultures. Through manipulating these levers, organizations may influence the desired culture. Many businesses have experienced incredible market turnarounds as a result of their efforts.

5.5 Collaboration, Communication, and Capability

These three crucial elements are crucial to the success of collaborative efforts. Good communication between parties is needed to fully comprehend each other's viewpoints and needs. Collaboration necessitates effective contact. Collaboration requires a willingness to share space with others to hear and accept their suggestions and ideas. Good communication and teamwork lead to innovation. There is no cooperation where there is only one-way communication; there is only enforcement, and compliance is barren ground for creating creative solutions.

Wise managers ensure that their employees are capable of interacting and collaborating efficiently, and these skills extend to all in the Change Unity Model.

To summarise, it is the duty of all project stakeholders to foster progress unity. To create and retain a shared focus, everyone must connect effectively with one another, cooperate to build the future, and assist one another in being capable of delivering their piece of the puzzle.

Moving beyond individualism to accomplish collective goals necessitates some sacrifice, but the benefits are larger and more long-term.

Commitment entails sticking to the plan and not allowing Distraction to obstruct the road to success.

A fun way for teams to remain focused is to keep track of how many times Distraction is resolved versus how many goals the team scores as a result. Keep a separate scorecard to track how often the team consciously focused on team unity to accomplish a goal and how often 'individualism' led to a loss.

5.6 Is Your Leadership Effective?

Strong leadership is difficult to describe in several respects. It's impossible to quantify. There is no "score" or "report card" for leadership. In reality, qualitative rather than quantitative measures of leadership are often used, while quantitative outcomes still follow. So, how can you say whether or not your leadership abilities are effective?

Simply put, leadership is the process of persuading others to take action. If a leader's effectiveness is missing, people will put in less than their best effort. The greater the initiative, the stronger the leadership.

Exceptional leadership motivates others to give their all.

Individual competencies and organizational culture both play a role in effective leadership. What are some indicators that a leader isn't being as successful as he or she should be? There are quite a few of them. They're signs that something in the leadership equation isn't quite right.

- Inability to Motivate People
- Difficulty Attracting/Retaining the Right People
- Low Productivity
- Poor Customer Orientation
- High Stress
- Isolation
- Declining Profits
- Ineffective Delegation
- Lack of Creativity
- Lack of Initiative
- Ineffective Teams
- Poor Communications

- Lack of Vision
- Diminishing Revenues
- High Turnover

What can be done to improve leadership effectiveness? The answer is simple to understand and yet not so simple to implement. It starts with understanding the foundations of what makes someone an effective leader and what kind of organizational culture is most effective.

Effective personal leadership can be summarized as being competent in these skill sets:

1. Becoming Influential
2. Facilitating Teamwork & Collaboration
3. Being a Catalyst for Change
4. Managing Conflict
5. Developing Others
6. Having & Communicating a Compelling Vision

5.7 The foundations of a strong organization are:

a. Developing a clear and compelling Purpose
b. Identifying the organization's Mission to achieve the Purpose
c. Agreeing on a set of Values by which to carry out the Mission
d. Adopting a Servant Leader attitude throughout the organization

In summary, when we combine personal competency in all areas of leadership skills with an organizational culture which supports people, their development, and their success, we end up with exceptional leadership which, in turn, inspires the best effort in others.

6 – CONFLICT MANAGEMENT: 6 TIPS TO SUCCESSFULLY MANAGE DISAGREEMENTS AT WORK

It is commonly known that when people work together or have some sort of relationship that requires them to make important decisions together, they will have disagreements and differences of opinion. There is no such thing as a "conflict-free" workplace.

How many of you have had a workplace conflict? Conflicts that make you wonder if you're in an adult workplace or a children's playground? I have, and I can assure you, my dear, that it is not a good feeling. The main thing is to learn how to handle such disputes so that everyone involved can function in a safer and healthier atmosphere.

If you're actually interested in or experiencing tension at work, I encourage you to continue reading. Six tips for effectively managing workplace disputes or conflicts are given below.

Following these simple tips will allow you to not only recognize when a dispute is brewing but also to effectively handle it to foster a better working relationship with your coworkers and a happier and more efficient working atmosphere for you and those around you.

Tip #1: Figure out what the "real" problem is: This is one of the most important suggestions. Make sure you understand what's causing the tension to begin with. You'll have a greater chance of attacking the real problem if you recognise it first, rather than wasting time trying to solve a problem that wasn't the real issue at the time.

Tip #2: Listen to what the other person has to say: Listen, listen, and listen more, once you've done listening. This is important. By listening to the other side, you will determine if you have the right case or whether the other person has a good point and you are the one who needs to "alter" the way the dispute is handled.

Tip #3: Express your point of view in a respectful way:: Don't be shy about expressing your thoughts or letting the other person know what you think. The trick is to approach it thoughtfully and respectfully.

Allowing your feelings to get in the way will make you appear to be a cry baby.

Tip # 4: Compromise: Work together to find a way to resolve the issue or come up with a different solution to the problem at hand. By compromising, you demonstrate to all parties interested in the issue that you value their input and that all you want is for the problem to be resolved. Have a "I don't want to win" mentality. It is preferable to bargain.

Tip # 5: Communicate with a supervisor: If after trying to solve the problem with all the parts involved you still feel that an agreement hasn't been reached, speak to your boss so he can be mindful of the situation and assist you in finding the right solution. But keep in mind that taking advice and complaining about your colleagues are not the same thing. When you go to speak with your boss, make sure you look professional and have all of your ducks in a row, or you'll come across as if you're pressuring him to take sides, which isn't a smart move.

Tip # 6: Learn from the experience and move on: Every conflict we encounter in our lives has the potential to teach us something. Make the most of those opportunities to learn something new and to be open to new ideas. This isn't to say that you shouldn't fight for what you believe is right, but it does mean that you should appreciate and learn from other people's perspectives and ideas. Then it's time to move on!

Managing disagreements successfully is an ability that not everyone has, but it is not difficult to master. It necessitates that one of the parties involved in the dispute determines that he or she does not want to continue arguing and instead wishes to resolve the conflict in the proper manner, while still deciding to behave like the "big child" to ensure a positive outcome during the conflict resolution process.

One last thought, "successful leaders manage conflict; they don't shy away from it or suppress it but see it as an engine of creativity and innovation. Some of the most creative ideas come out of people in conflict remaining in conversation with one another rather than flying into their own corners or staking out entrenched positions. The challenge for leaders is to develop structures and processes in which such conflicts can be orchestrated productively."

6.1 Common Reasons For Team-Building

In my 27 years of team-building with groups I have interviewed many executives as they contemplate the decision to hold some type of team development program. From shorter, lighter, fun programs to in-depth interventions for really stuck teams the goals for team building vary widely or can often be inadequately defined.

Most clients are not team building experts, but they describe the signs of poor coordination as a lack of communication, lack of confidence, redundancy of effort, or a lack of progress where it is most needed because this or that workgroup isn't 'moving along.' It is frequently a very beneficial experience for them to have the consultant help that determine precisely what the challenges are and what desired teamwork solutions are feasible. I always assist my clients in determining what is actually going on with their team and what they really want, rather than how they are currently handling one another.

Some of the most common reasons given by companies for engaging in a team-building programme are as follows:

1) Have Fun

For some cause, some people just want to have a good time. While almost any team experience can be used to teach useful teamwork skills, having fun is often the goal. Organizations may already have extensive training and development programmes in place and simply want to take a break from it all, or simply want to have a nice time. This may be affected by the organization's atmosphere as well as inexperienced or inept leadership. Without passing judgement, it's worth noting that a high-energy shared experience has a number of advantages, including allowing people to see each other in a different light than at work, creating a relaxed environment in which people can feel more comfortable talking to someone at a higher level in the organization, and bonding with one another through a shared activity such as a softball game.

Any longer-term benefits will inevitably occur if standards for building teamwork are low and results are not established, but not generally the highest priority benefits that a workgroup will need.

2) Gather everybody and share your experience.

Shared events, which are often organized by well-intentioned people, should ideally take into account each person's level of comfort and involvement. For others, rock climbing, for example, can be an intense trust-building activity, while for others, it can be an embarrassing reminder of one's lack of physical fitness. The goal is to define the group culture and create a sense of belonging by doing something together. Typical examples include going on a dinner cruise together, engaging in corporate Olympics or business picnic-type activities, and so on. Any activity in which everybody is in the same place doing the same thing will help to cement the concept of 'the team' or 'the community.'

While this is a simple goal, many businesses are unable to seek deeper meaning or learn because they are afraid of cultural backlash if they do not do anything 'cool enough' to keep each clique and faction satisfied.

Of course, there is no limit on how much money can be spent on lavish activities, but many of them have little long-term intrinsic value to the team when everyone returns to the same way of working together the next week. These kinds of activities are more like gifts to keep employees happy than opportunities to learn and develop as a team.

3) Celebrate Recent Achievements

This form of a team event, although similar to number 2 above, has more structure and content and serves a very useful function for the team. The following are some main points:

- Acknowledging that everybody has been working hard, thus validating the reason for regularly demanding a lot of staff.
- Acknowledge that the strategy succeeded and that the objectives were met. This instils trust in the leadership and fosters support and confidence in the progress of future initiatives.
- Awards praise and acknowledgement to those who merit it. Most workers yearn to be recognised for their efforts and to be considered as respected member of the team.
- Helps to develop a sense of self as a member of a powerful, competent, and effective team.

4) Presented or Perceived as a Workplace/Company Benefit

Again, a 'perk' for working for a specific company may be a luxury road trip or junket that is marketed as team building, but is really a personal advantage that many workers look forwards to because of the great food, resort hotel, and remote location. Some workplace environments offer these types of benefits regularly, but few have a genuine teambuilding structure.

More often than not, they're packed with extra revenue or technological training, or they're used to reveal next year's targets, which are meant to go down with the spoonful of sugar that the opulent junket helps to provide. It's not always easy to combine recalculating next year's sales or development targets with team building.

5) Interact with Senior Management, Key Customers or Vendors

Team building can be a good way to force interaction to cement relationships. This can seem ingenious at first, but well-structured team bonding programmes are an excellent way to deepen business relationships, which must first be suitable personal relationships. A shared activity like a ropes course or team initiative activities will open up and inspire all sorts of experiences and conversation, bringing people closer together. Teamwork can be strengthened in the value chain by improving communication and cooperation, learning about one another's leadership and decision-making styles, and exploring strategic approaches to quality and improvement in enjoyable ways together.

6) Encourage team members to communicate with one another.

Any community can improve its contact with each other. It's the most popular team-building goal, and it's almost always at the core of what colleagues want to improve when they return to work.

All great team building programmes should include modelling group communication skills.

7) Cooperation/Collaboration between two groups

This is a common justification for team building initiatives, and it should be used more often, particularly when two workgroups or divisions are critical parts of the value chain, such as sales and development, or engineering and marketing. Each group must gain a better understanding of the other's needs and capabilities, and work towards a reasonable set of expectations that promotes productivity and a way of doing business that everyone can live with, especially the customer. Often a lot of healing and dispute resolution is needed, as well as a healthy dose of enrolling everyone in better ways to get stuff done in the future.

8) Acquisition or merger

When an organization's structures and infrastructure shift, everybody wonders how it will affect them. If they've gotten past the question of whether they'll still have a job, the next reasonable questions are about what each employee's position and duties will be, and how things will vary on a day-to-day basis.

Employees want guarantees. Will the status quo be kept, or will major policy and practice changes be implemented? How will the improvements be implemented? While calling this "team-building" is a stretch, it is often necessary to bring everyone together to communicate a new strategy or concept, to rapidly integrate operations and new requirements with no interruption in development. It's a classic organizational challenge, but one that a well-designed team building programme will help with. After all, the modern must coexist with the old to produce a stronger and more competent outcome.

These team-building activities must be carefully planned.

9) A new management/leadership team is in place.

Many military organizations are plagued by command changes every two years or so. Each new commander aspires to leave an indelible mark and make a difference unlike any other.

These commanders understand that they must rapidly create a new speed and atmosphere, unite high-level influencers and important departments into an even more powerful machine, and steer the machine towards ever-higher targets. Everyone involved dreads the introduction of a new commander and tries to stay under the radar to avoid being heard or seen as a chance for advancement or transition. The private sector lacks the military's role specificity and rigidity of structure, but makes up for it with political intrigue, the emergence of ambiguity, and a lack of humanity.

A great incentive to participate in a team-building programme is to integrate new leadership and a "new approach." Instead of any detached and ambitious management by goals strategy by an executive who hasn't been there and done that, the secret to success is to concentrate on what works now, the voice of the worker, preparation for change, and consensus on areas that need improvement.

A team-building initiative will be used for one of its highest possible advantages by a humble new boss who listens rather than says, who tries to understand rather than redefines, and who uses subtlety rather than a command to institute a new flow.

10) Work together to develop a new strategy and direction.

When this motivation is real, it has the potential to be extremely strong. Before telling everyone to get on the latest bandwagon with them, top management should hopefully know where they're heading.

They must have concrete plans and be unambiguous in their determination. In this case, the message to employers and staff is to inspire them to help the leadership team that knows how to get out of the current situation or crisis. If these types of team-building strategies aren't well-thought-out and implemented, they'll fall flat. The message sent to workers in this situation is that we will band together to get through this crisis and that we will support and collaborate to get things done.

Employees easily detect deceptive lip service and a lack of dedication from key executives who do not lead by example and place their money where their mouth is.

11) The dysfunctional group

Since dysfunctional organizations are made up of dysfunctional people, changing the group's modus operandi would necessitate a set of individual behavioural adjustments. This is a truly sophisticated process requiring very sophisticated methods to get the group to want to commit to a new strategy, to see something in it for them to act differently together individually and collectively, and to let go of ego-based defences and negative attitudes that interrupt the work group's smooth functioning.

This work group's chaotic existence usually costs the business a lot of money and frustrates those around them. Furthermore, most people in the company are afraid to discuss the obvious, challenge unproductive habits, and recommend that these people raise their game for the sake of everyone's well-being.

The problems are viewed like political hot potatoes or discussed in hushed tones or unnecessarily sensitive terms because of 'who they are' in the corporate hierarchy, rather than being branded as the immature, unprofessional, inefficient, and ludicrous activities that they are. Everyone agrees that there is a simpler way of doing things out there if only they were willing to consider it. Herein lies the stumbling block. The whole aim of the team building experience is to facilitate dedication to move past the current state to a better future state, and it requires very qualified and competent handling. The prospect of a more rewarding way of operating, like a fragile baby chick emerging from its shell, must be treated with care. New ideas must be carefully presented and subscribed to, with very clear standards about how they will be implemented on everyone's part. To overcome a history of mistrust and move forwards together towards a more collaborative, transparent, and truthful future, each group member must be seen to make this decision and agreement. This is where the finest art of facilitated team building can be found.

A community like this would frequently need ongoing counselling for a period of time to be reminded of their dedication to avoid reverting to old behavioural patterns.

Corporate team building programmes may have a wide range of objectives or a variety of objectives, necessitating a versatile, tailored approach. The aim is to achieve results: a better-functioning, happier, and more efficient work team, whether on the front lines or at the top of the corporate ladder. At every level of the company, people are people, and they often need the strength and leverage of a well-designed team bonding programme to remind them that they can still work together, and even enjoy it.

EXERCISE

WRITE DOWN METHODS IN WHICH YOU CAN MANAGE DISAGREEMENT AT WORK AS A LEADER

7 – ALWAYS THE VICTIM AT WORK? WIN WITH FEEDBACK

Anyone who sets boundaries with others is now labelled as 'controlling,' according to a new workplace pattern. It's whispered between managers after performance review meetings with staff, and it's said at the water cooler during gossip sessions.

How do we create boundaries at work without being labelled as "controlling"? What would we do to avoid being dumped on, dismissed, or shunned? What would we do to avoid being victims?

Effective communication is one weapon at your disposal. Learn how to provide constructive feedback during your professional performance assessment meetings with your manager. This is a skill you should develop, and here are some reasons why you should.

Boundaries are set by companies all of the time.

Google defines feedback as providing "information about a person's performance of a task" with the intention of using it as a "basis for change." In 1980s management jargon, the term "feedback" was used to describe how customers felt about a business. As businesses realised that the majority of the feedback they were receiving was about specific employees, they set up employee appraisal meetings to learn more about customer/company relationships.

Grunig's 'Public Relations Feedback Model' shows why companies don't have to treat their consumers as strangers. Customers have an emotional attachment to the goods and services they buy. A four-way model was used to monitor customer satisfaction levels, in which an Initiator/Sender initiates contact about their experience with the business somewhere or somehow.

Similarly, realise that when your supervisor asks you to provide input about the organization during your performance assessment meeting, you are being placed in the role of Initiator (Stage One) of the feedback model.

If you want to advance in your career, you must understand that being assigned to Stage One of the communications models means you will be providing information to a specific audience (your boss). Whatever you suggest during a performance evaluation is normally not kept private and will be shared with "higher-ups."

THE PR FEEDBACK MODEL IS Regulated BY COMPANIES.

A Stage One message is transmitted by word of mouth, the media, a smartphone, or, recently social media. Step two of the model consists of a Sender (in the case of performance appraisals - YOU) who transmits the message (via talking, telephone, computer message forum, etc.).

What do you think a company can do with the Senders in Stage Two of the model?

The organization begins profiling employee responses as a result of the answer. You may have completed a personality questionnaire or a test to assess your job style, learning style, Myers Briggs personality, or something else. This will be suggested at some stage (especially if you work in a large company). The profiling information on you will be used by your bosses to obtain input about the business. Open-ended questions are used by bosses to elicit specific responses from you. It won't be as straightforward as asking, "How are you finding things?"

'How simple is it to get information from accounts each month when you need it?' is an example of how company targeting is used to frame questions that sound personal and attacking. In this case, the organization has profile intelligence gleaned from interviews with account personnel. So, if you're asked a question like this, where do you think it came from? Reading between the lines, it seems that someone in accounts has sent you input on how they dealt with you. How does your manager know there's an issue with the books?

Beware Dishonesty in Performance Appraisals

It's possible that you've previously complained (perhaps loudly enough for anyone else to hear) that account service is sluggish. It's a good idea to tread carefully at this stage because it's important to be truthful - but you're in a performance assessment meeting.

Saying 'it's all right now' because you're afraid of getting in trouble for whining isn't going to endear you to a manager who has just discovered two accounts workers have gone on long-term sick leave, and other staff have expressed concerns during appraisals. You'll have to speak out about the difficulties you're having.

Stage 3: You're the Boss - What is your level of familiarity with them?

Navigating Stage three of the model is needed for effective feedback. Someone (the Receiver) receives a message, and the company must be able to capture it. Your manager is the receiver in performance assessment sessions. This could be the best way to prepare for a performance review meeting. It's a good idea to write down every problem you've brought to your boss's attention in the last month or so, as well as how the issue was handled. You don't want to come off as someone who has never received support or assistance.

Consider concerns that you know others have raised and how they were handled. Giving feedback that is compatible with other team members, whether positive or negative, is much easier. If the manager has made a good effort to deal with the problem, as in our example with accounts, you can provide constructive feedback. 'I've learned there's a staffing shortage there, so I'm afraid what we can anticipate are delays,' for example. I'm sure they're giving it their all.

7.1 The meeting's fourth stage is to end on a positive note.

An organization must be able to ask itself whether clarification has been reached to effectively complete Stage four. When it comes to performance review sessions, managers are often told to finish on a good note. Was the product we released this year a hit? Are we able to satisfy the needs of our customers? Was the service deemed satisfactory? Are you happy with your job?

The fact that these questions are asked with the personal pronoun could make you nervous. "How can you say you satisfy consumer demands?" and

"How nice is your customer service?" seem to imply that there has been a complaint. Consider how much simpler it is to be constructive when the question isn't personal: "How do you think the business serves customers the best?" Before you panic, remember that what you're actually being asked is how well the company has prepared you for consumer needs and services, as well as how comfortable you are providing service to customers. Consider the following scenario: "Why do you think the business serves consumers the best?" If it helps, you can plan by mentally rephrasing questions before the meeting.

7.2 Maintain Self-Control and Get Positive Feedback

An organization gets the majority of its input by controlled questioning of its staff, rather than tracking every social media site on the planet. It doesn't have to be difficult to give input at work. Learn the rules of the game. You should smile to yourself the next time someone describes someone else as "a little controlling." When it comes to performance appraisals, the majority of us keep our cool.

Remember that companies collect feedback through customer surveys, supplier questionnaires, and media monitoring campaigns. All of these outlets may be used to question you during performance reviews. Note, they're more interested in the company's performance than in you personally.

7.3 Useful Tips for Giving Good Feedback to Staff

"Tell me how you'll judge me, and I'll tell you how I'll act," says an old business adage. This emphasises the importance of feedback in day-to-day business operations.

Employees may be "course-corrected" using feedback if they are performing more productively and in line with management's priorities.

Employees will also be encouraged to keep up the good work by receiving feedback.

Understanding how to give good feedback is important because:

- ✓ It stops small issues become large, disruptive ones
- ✓ It helps build trust in working relationships
- ✓ It promotes professional and personal growth
- ✓ It acknowledges individual and team achievements
- ✓ It resolves any misunderstandings

Being able to give effective feedback improves employee productivity, morale and makes the workplace more enjoyable and rewarding.

How to Give Good Feedback

Feedback should be supportive and helpful.

Always make sure the person is expecting feedback and is prepared to receive it. Before giving your feedback, it's a good idea to ask them for their opinion on the situation. Not only should feedback be positive and constructive, but it should also not be used to chastise workers.

Be specific and sincere in your responses.

It's important to keep feedback objective at all times. Keep the focus on the real action you saw rather than personality characteristics. "You're way too chatty!" may be rephrased as "I noticed you were away from your desk for extended periods of time and I'm concerned about your productivity." Avoid making ambiguous statements or inferences.

Be sincere.

Use "I saw...I heard...I thought" phrases. Describe how the behaviour impacts you and convey your message with honesty. If you don't believe the compliment was well-deserved, don't offer it.

Maintain a healthy balance

Often strive to have a blend of positive and constructive feedback. Ending with a constructive comment and encouraging an answer to the feedback is often preferable. It's important to remember that it's much easier to demotivate someone than it is to inspire them.

Ensure that you receive timely feedback.

If feedback is given too long after the situation under review, it loses its effectiveness and becomes negative. Don't hold back any kind of input, and try to send it as soon as possible after the case.

Giving Positive Remarks

When someone does something good, positive feedback is given. Positive feedback can be provided in a very simple way:

Describe what the person did or said in detail.

Explain why this action was successful.

Ascertain that the "What" and "Why" methods incorporate the above-mentioned points. "Here's an example: "I am extremely pleased with your progress report and review. It was simple and succinct, and it addressed a range of issues that I will address. You did an excellent job."

Providing constructive criticism

Similar to positive feedback a good approach for feedback for improvement (remember - not "negative feedback"!) is:

- Describe what the person did or said in detail.
- Clearly show a more successful strategy.
- Explain why you think that would have been a safer option.

Consider the following scenario: "Your remarks about the progress report came across as cynical and too broad to be helpful, in my opinion. We will really benefit from your feedback if you keep your reports objective and communicate your questions clearly and concisely "..

Any of the suggestions above will help you develop your team leadership skills and supervisory management strategies, as well as inspire and guide your employees.

Give Efficient & Effective Feedback

Giving someone feedback (in both a personal and professional setting) is something we all do daily. It is important to provide continuous feedback to those around us at work to build better relationships, enhance company performance, and enable others to grow and develop. Although we are constantly giving feedback, many of us give it incorrectly! When you give feedback in the wrong way, you risk having the opposite outcome you expected, and in some situations, you risk ruining your relationship with the other person.

Keep the following tips in mind the next time you give input to an employee, coworker, boss, or even a spouse or family member:

Share your desire to provide the feedback:

This will give the other individual time to prepare for it, and they will be less defensive as a result. You should also avoid providing feedback when someone is not in the right state of mind to accept it - for example, when they are busy, exhausted, frustrated, or depressed.

When you tell them you want to share something, they will be able to tell you whether it is a good time or not.

Make sure it's timely:

Don't wait for your quarterly review to bring up everything that happened in the second quarter! Not only do you risk the feedback no longer being applicable, but taking too long to provide feedback on a problem allows you to forget some of the facts of the case, making your argument less relevant and making you less trustworthy as the feedback provider.

Have the proper setting:

Giving positive feedback in front of a group of people can be beneficial at times, but in most situations, finding a private place where you can be alone is preferable. This will promote a conversation and show the other person that you value the conversation enough to make time for it.

Give your undivided attention and treat others with respect:

First and foremost, keep your dedication if you have a structured meeting planned (such as a quarterly discussion with an employee). If you keep rescheduling it, or even forget about it and don't show up, it sends the message to the other person that "this isn't important to me!" Also, give the other person your undivided attention - try to block out any other distractions (cell phone, e-mail, shut your door) and let them know this is your top priority right now.

Don't make broad generalisations:

It's important to be able to include precise information for your message to be properly handled. If the other person just gave an excellent presentation, tell them what made it so. They'll be able to replicate the desired behaviour the next time, and they'll know you're sincerely invested rather than only providing input for the sake of providing it.

Combine the "what" and "why" into one sentence:

It's one thing to tell someone what they did; it's another to explain why it's relevant enough to mention. If your boss fails to adequately communicate her department's plans with you, explain why this is an issue for you; your input can have a much greater effect.

Invite a response and pay attention:

Nothing is more frustrating than being told you don't do anything well and then being denied the opportunity to express your opinion; you typically leave feeling disappointed and angry. To avoid this happening with the person you're giving feedback to, always ask for a response; this will start a conversation. Who knows, you may not have all of the facts straight, and this will give them the opportunity to correct you and prevent a major misunderstanding.

Thank them for their generosity:

Often express gratitude to the other person for expressing their thoughts on the input you provided. It establishes confidence and invites them to participate in a feedback session with you in the future. Even if you disagree with their answer, letting them know you appreciate it (and that you welcome a healthy dialogue) will make future sessions much more productive.

Applying these helpful ideas each time you give someone feedback will ensure your message is properly received and that you get the results you desire.

8 – FIGHT FEAR OF SUCCESS AND FEAR OF FAILURE!

Fear is a common obstacle to achieving goals, keeping New Year's resolutions, and fulfilling dreams. We are afraid of something we don't comprehend. We are afraid of being humiliated or ashamed. We're afraid of making and breaking the same New Year's promise over and over. We are averse to transition. We are afraid of getting hit. Fear comes in a variety of shapes and sizes, and it affects us all. It's an irrational and sometimes emotional reaction to life. Since it's so natural to exaggerate stuff when you're scared, it's frequently larger than life.

Fear is an unpleasant sensation, and we often avoid fun, enjoyable experiences because we are 'afraid.' It's easy to avoid dating or romantic relationships if you've been hurt in romance often enough. It's easy to lose confidence and openness when it comes to feelings and emotions. Similarly, if you burn your hand on a burner, you try not to do it again because it hurts. True, dealing with a fear of burning your hand on a stove is easier than dealing with a fear of losing a relationship.

I bring them up because they depict two very different, but equally popular, types of 'fear.'

So, how do you escape "fear of failure and fear of success" while pursuing a dream or contemplating "taking the leap of faith" and pursuing a dream? There is no one-size-fits-all solution, but here are some ideas based on common sense:

Recognize when 'fear' is getting in the way of a dream or 'stalling' it. A person's fear of failure can paralyze them. Perhaps you're afraid of 'failing again' because you keep making the same mistake. Perhaps it's time to seek the guidance of a trusted friend, counselor, or instructor who can look at the situation objectively and without emotion. Much better if you seek advice from an 'expert.' For example, if you're trying to lose weight, a personal trainer will assist you in developing an exercise routine that suits your needs. Don't try to do it on your own. Seek advice.

Recognize when a lack of 'intelligence' or 'skill' is the source of 'fear.' This plays into the fear of failure once more. You'll have more influence over your course of action, and each and every step you take towards achieving your goal, if you educate yourself before you start working on it - and continue the education process throughout your journey. From a place of strength and bravery, you may move forwards. Information is a powerful tool!

Recognize when 'fear of success' is preventing you from achieving your goals. Success also brings about both big and minor changes in a person's life. It's easy to be afraid of 'change itself,' rather than enjoying the successes, satisfaction, fun, pleasure, and enjoyment. If we like it or not, change is inevitable. Why not welcome improvement into your life by following a long-held ambition? The worst that can happen is that you'll make mistakes along the way, or that you'll realize the dream isn't really your cup of tea. If this occurs, remember your lessons and carry on!

Recognize that 'fear' can exaggerate the true nature of a situation; it's not all "all in your head." What's the worst that can happen if you follow your dreams? Unless, of course, your dream is to climb a mountain and you fall off a cliff, most mistakes won't kill you. But, even if climbing the mountain is your fantasy, don't let fear hold you back. Learn everything you can on how to climb the mountain safely, and do everything you can to protect yourself. If reaching the 'highest peak' is really your goal, don't go to your grave without attempting it!

Recognize that this is the last chance. You just get one chance to live your dreams in this world. Why live a life filled with remorse and sorrow for all the things you 'didn't do' but desperately wanted to 'try'? Fear is a major deterrent to having a good night's sleep. Don't let it hold you down. Don't fall for it!

I struggle with both fear of failure and fear of success. It's in our essence. However, if you want to climb mountains, write books, run marathons, or aim for the stars, you must first identify, embrace, and appreciate fear, then move on with your hopes, resolutions, and goals. No one, including myself, claims to have all the answers. Every day, I learn something different, and that is what keeps me going. I aspire to learn new things, to overcome my fears, and to 'fight' for my hopes, resolutions, and goals. Then I rejoice in my successes and push onward once more!

8.1 Fighting Fear

Fear is a normal reaction to change. We take a step into the unknown when we adjust. We can't prepare for any contingency no matter how well we intend. And therein lies the difficulty.

All can be shifted by a single change.

We instinctively understand that when we partake in a phase of transition in our lives, even if it is a minor one, it affects everything around us. Even if it's limited to a single arena, a big enough change can have a ripple impact in our lives.

Outer Change Effects Inner Change

This is because all of the improvements we create in our outside world have an effect on who we are on the inside. Our behaviors, assumptions, and beliefs are influenced by how we want to behave in or respond to the world around us. When the heart of who we are changes, anything else we affect changes as well. That is to say, transition poses a threat to everything we have now.

We can lose things, people, and relationships that are important to us if we change.

Fear Of Loss

When viewed from this perspective, we can see that the anxiety we're dealing with is a fear of loss rather than a fear of the unknown. We don't want to risk what we have because we fear that what comes in its place will be worse. When it comes to this point, even the most passionate optimists seem to lose confidence.

Giving Up Doesn't Always Mean Loss

We don't know that by making a different choice for our lives, we are changing who we are. Any improvements brought on by the shift would be a direct product of the new things we want. So if people, relationships, objects, careers, and other aspects of our lives fade away after that, it's because we wanted them to.

However, It Can Be Frustrating

That doesn't make it any less unpleasant. Grief is almost always present in the aftermath of a loss. However, it is a loss that we have chosen. When we are considering improvement, this reality seems to elude us. Most people believe that if they make different decisions and change the world around them, they will be completely out of reach.

How Can Most People Overcome Their Fears?

As a result, most people eventually partake in the process of transition because they either become hopeful about what the change can offer, or, more often, they decide that nothing can be worse than what they already have. In fact, we often discover that the best cure for fear is experience. We feel more secure when we have prior experience with something so we know (or believe we know) what to expect.

Overcoming Fear: The Real Deal

But, if we're being honest, there's no way of knowing what to expect. There are far too many factors to consider. The key to overcoming fear in any situation is to believe in yourself, your ability to adapt, and your willingness to look after yourself along the way. This is, in the end, the best solution. Surrendering and believing that the higher power will take care of you is also beneficial if you believe in a benevolent higher power.

Fear in a Parable

I've been working on a personal development book. There's a part of it that I figured you would find useful today. As a parting thought, I'll leave you with this.

A woman who was unable to overcome her fears prayed to the spirits for assistance. "Why, oh spirits, am I trapped, unable to pass, despite my wishes to take giant leaps forwards?" The spirits responded by passing their hands over the fabric of her vision.

Threads emerged where their hands passed, more threads than she had ever seen in her life, running in all directions and crossing at seemingly random locations. The majority of the threads converged on her.

"So I am bound" she said. "Who has done this to me? And how do I get loose of these bonds?"

"No one has done this to you" answered the spirits. "This is the nature of who you are. All of life is connected through these cords that you see around you. If you were to be loosed of your bonds, you would cease to exist in this world."

"I don't understand" she said.

"Try moving" they replied. She moved her arm and saw that, as she did, some cords flexed and moved easily, and others were already stretched taut and resisted her movement. She moved her leg and the same thing happened again.

"The ones that resist are the threads that connect you to people, ideas, assumptions and beliefs that hold you in place. You must either break those cords or remain where you are. The choice is yours."

She moved her arm again and watched how that movement rippled outwards across the web of cords that surrounded her. She moved her finger and saw that even that movement affected the whole. She realized that each cord was not just loosely attached. Some pulled in one direction or another. Some were comfortable, others itched and burned. Some cords twisted tightly around one another, others existed almost in isolation. She could not imagine what would happen if she broke a cord.

"The web you see around you is the web of your life. If you break a strand, the rest of your life must adjust to compensate. Some changes have little effect, others change the nature of the web. You are stuck in fear because you are unwilling to accept the changes to your web that your choices would create. That too is a choice, but one we fear you may not be happy within the end."

"I understand," said the woman. And before she could change her mind, she cut the strands that chafed, the ones that burned, and the ones that held her in place. She made a choice to change - and her web was never the same again."

8.2 Remove the Fear of Taking Action

Feeling down, doubting your capacity, and, most importantly, being afraid of doing things that are outside of your comfort zone are all signs of a lack of self-confidence. Self-assurance is a necessary component of performance. According to a study by Cox (1998), boosting self-confidence by supportive comments, whether made by others or by myself, increases the probability of a person performing a task that is thought to be impossible. According to the report, the absence of anxiety is the main cause. When people are secure in what they are doing, they are able to overcome fear, which is the archrival of trust. Fear is what prevents people from doing things that are outside of their comfort zone. Fear is a powerful sensory sensation that affects the entire physiological process.

It's a natural instinct for us as animals. However, this does not imply that we will be able to solve it.

Let us attempt to describe the anatomy of fear as a barrier to achieving self-confidence. When faced with a potentially dangerous situation, fear is a normal human response. Fear is derived from a portion of the lower brain shared by humans and animals, according to scientific studies. It causes the body to release adrenaline and other emergency hormones to fight or flee from danger. The higher cerebral portion of the brain (which is responsible for higher thinking) will cease to function when this part of the brain takes over, allowing the lower brain to take charge of the body. It's no surprise that a defensive individual is similar to a turtle or a fleeing bunny fleeing from its predator.

Is it possible for us to exert control over our lower brain so that it does not control us? How do we overcome our fears and gain self-assurance? Here are some of the steps you can take to boost your self-esteem.

1. Control Your Reaction

Controlling our individual reaction is the first step towards complete self-confidence. We must be mindful of how our bodies function to do so. Take, for example, our ability to breathe. You can monitor intervals if you are conscious of them. There are also several yogis who have the ability to regulate their blood pressure or heart rate. The interconnectedness of our neural impulses is the explanation for this. Since our bodies and brains are connected by a network of nerves, we may be able to regulate automatic physiological functions such as heart rate and blood flow.

Being aware of your reaction will help you avoid doing things that are potentially harmful. It's one way to keep the lower brain from taking over again. One way to practice regulating your response is to do a quick breathing exercise. You can regulate the amount of oxygen you take in and calm your body by being mindful of your breathing.

2. Evaluate Your Fear

Once you've resolved your physical reaction, you'll need to process it in your higher brain. This can be accomplished by self-reflection or self-evaluation. Fearlessness allows you to analyze situations critically without being hampered by bodily reactions. As a result, you've silenced the voice of your lower brain, which only has two options: fight or flight.

3. Create a very Big Goal

You've resisted using your lower brain to express yourself when you evaluate your anxiety. As a result, you'll be inundated with millions of options. As a result, your higher brain will take control of your reasoning and lead you to more options in the situation. It is a morale booster to consider different options. The body will follow you as you begin to consider the possibilities, while the higher brain creates constructive sensory feedback for your body.

4. Chunk Your Goals to milestones

As you succeed in overcoming your lack of self-confidence, the next step is to break down your target into smaller chunks. A thousand miles of travel progresses in every move, according to Lao Tse. This is also true of our objectives. With a major target in mind, creating milestones will not confuse you. Instead, it will improve your self-confidence to accomplish a larger objective.

5. Create a habit of Success

The most crucial step on the path to complete self-assurance is to develop a winning habit. This can be accomplished by completing the milestones one at a time. You would be able to build a constructive outlook on things that you should do in this manner. Your optimistic outlook would be reinforced if you are consistent in reaching goals.

6. Stick to your goal

As you progress through the stages of gaining self-confidence, you are more likely to be enticed by other ambitions that are unrelated to your current target. It is impossible to serve two masters at the same time. Concentrate all of your energies on achieving your objective. As a result, your attention would not be spent on items that are unrelated to your objectives.

7. Accept defeat as a temporary setback and work your way back to victory.

Self-anti-hero confidence is a failure. Your chances of failing or failing to achieve your target are just as good as your chances of succeeding. On the other side, a loss can be used to your benefit. It's an opportunity to assess yourself. It's also a chance for you to defend yourself against a potential threat to your success. When confronted with loss, most people will focus on the situation and avoid worrying about how to win the next time. Michael Jordan once said that the number of shots he misses outnumbers the number of shots he makes.

Thomas Edison produced 99 light bulbs without success, but his 100th work was a success. Failures and misses are possible, but they can be managed once they've been assessed. You would be able to protect yourself from struggling to gain absolute self-confidence in this manner.

EXERCISE

PUT ALL THE PIECES OF THE PUZZLE AND MAKE SURE
YOU ANSWER THESE QUESTIONS?

Will I still be able to breathe in and breathe out at the end of the day if it
fails?

Have I thoroughly looked at all angles of the dream objectively?

How can I train my mind to overcome fear?

CONCLUSION

When learning how to start a conversation, you must first start with the basics. There are three basic elements of communication, according to communication experts. The message is the first component. The second component is a person who can send a message to another person, and the third is someone who can receive a message. Although it is true that messages are sent from one person to another on a daily basis, this does not mean that they are all understood or accurate. When learning about workplace communication, you must understand how to deliver a message in such a way that the recipient fully comprehends the meaning and purpose of the message. Conversations, whether verbal, nonverbal or written, can become more difficult at this stage. By learning how to initiate a conversation, you can prevent the difficulties that can arise while communicating at work.

Success in the workplace involves more than just being able to complete the tasks that have been assigned to you. You must be able to quickly approach people and initiate conversations, possess a high degree of likability, demonstrate a high level of self-confidence, leave a lasting impression, talk to practically everyone, and effectively develop long-term relationships. There is a clear connection between performance and social skills, according to studies. Yes, you read that correctly. You can reach a high degree of professional success simply by learning how to effectively socialise and communicate with others. Not only that, but your professional performance will spill over into your personal life! We've all met someone who seems to be liked by everyone. Their personalities function like magnets, attracting people, prosperity, and happiness in a moment. What is the key to their success? They understand how to strike up a conversation. You can now do the same!

The first rule of enhancing organizational communication is to simply be friendly. People who are friendly are respected and paid attention to. This is due to the fact that people are interested in what they have to suggest. The next rule for starting a conversation is to show genuine interest in the other person. What are their recommendation? What are their hopes and expectations? What is crucial to them? Avoid being the "talker" at all costs. Take a step back and consider yourself a "listener." The most critical part of a conversation, according to communication experts, is what is said rather than what is said. You can converse more than if you were talking if you listen. While this may seem strange, it is the reality. Last but not least, don't put any of the blame for the conversation on yourself. It's a two-way street when it comes to communication. You can't have a conversation by yourself. You are more likely to have good workplace contact if you relieve yourself of stress. Following these basic tactics, you'll soon discover that learning how to initiate a conversation isn't a difficult task, but rather an enjoyable one that can lead to high levels of success in both your personal and professional life.

Do not go yet; One last thing to do

If you enjoyed this book or found it useful, I'd be very grateful if you'd post a short review on it. Your support really does make a difference and I read all the reviews personally so I can get your feedback and make this book even better.

Thanks again for your support!

Made in United States
Orlando, FL
06 December 2021

11245051R00065